Dad School

A Field Guide to Happiness

By: Pop

Editor: Kalli Groce
Hotwash: Roland Minez

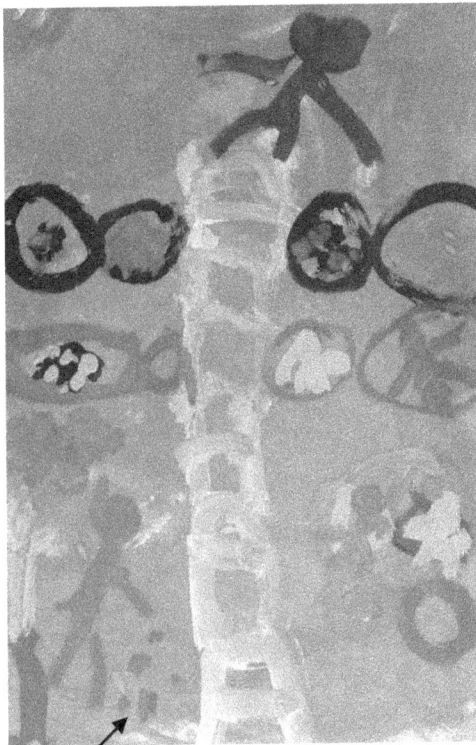

"blood"

"Mom Falling Off a Ladder and
Breaking Her Arm"

- Boo, age 6, Senegal

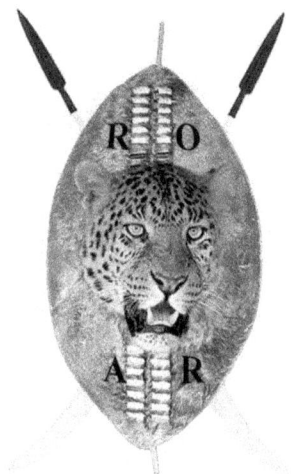

R O

A R

CONTENTS

I

THE DAD SCHOOL DOJO

Boo, Kidogo, Little Bear and Pips,

On 25 December 1923, a 29-year-old boxer named Billy Miske spent a cold Christmas smiling and laughing with his wife and three kids at his warm home in St. Paul, Minn. The next morning, Billy woke, called his manager, Jack Reddy, and said, "Come get me Jack. I'm dying."

Five years earlier, doctors told Billy that he only had five years to live. He had Bright's disease, which causes the kidneys to fail. They told him to stop boxing, because if he continued, it would kill him. Billy, however, was only 24 years old. He was also a good fighter, his business was $100,000 in debt and he had to support his wife and three young kids.

Given this, Billy decided not to tell anyone except Jack Reddy that he was sick. Instead, he decided to keep fighting, pay off his debt and take care of his family.

Five years later, when Death was supposed to have come collected the debt on Billy's borrowed life, Billy had fought 29 more times. He'd fought some big fights too, against monster fighters like Tommy Gibbons, Harry Greb and Jack Dempsey. His record was 50-8-3, which included the 29 fights while terminally ill.

In Dempsey's autobiography, Dempsey wrote, "My first defense of the World Heavyweight Title was on Labor Day 1920, against a friend of mine. I didn't know his condition was as bad as it was. All I knew was that he begged me for the fight. He was broke and needed a good payday to regain his health. I knocked him out because I loved the guy."

By the fall of 1923, Billy was really sick. He was close to dying and knew it. Remarkably, he'd paid off his debt, which equates to over $1,300,000 today, but Christmas was coming and he hardly had anything left. He couldn't buy presents for his kids.

So Billy told Jack to get him a fight. Jack refused. If you go in the ring now, Jack said, you'll die. Billy persisted, so Jack said, "Well, train for a while then, and if you can put on some weight, I'll see what I can do." Billy said that he couldn't do that, because he was too weak to train, and he'd be dead by then.

So Jack conceded. He got Billy the only fight he could, against "KO" Bill Brennan. Brennan weighed over 200 pounds and had fought several title fights, including one against Dempsey, in which he went 12 rounds — 9 rounds longer than Billy had.

The fight was scheduled for 7 November 1923, in Omaha, Nebraska. Billy didn't train. He didn't prepare. He didn't do anything, because he couldn't. Mostly, he just stayed in bed and ate boiled fish.

The day of the fight, Billy got to Omaha and into the ring. His legs were weak, but he didn't tell anyone. He survived the first round. The second. The third. In all, he went four rounds and got paid $2,400.

That Christmas, which he knew was his last, Billy made it the best his family had ever seen. He stacked the tree with presents for his kids, filled the house with food and bought a baby grand piano for his wife. Years later, his kids remembered that day fondly, smiling and laughing.

The morning after Christmas, Billy called Jack. He told Jack to come get him, because he was dying. Jack took him to the hospital. Billy died a few days later, on New Year's Day 1924.

Rick Reilly wrote a good article about this story in Sports Illustrated in 1999.[1] It's paraphrased here. One of the best parts about the story, though, has to do with that last fight Billy had, with KO Bill Brennan in Omaha. You see, Billy won the fight. He beat KO Bill Brennan. In four rounds. By a knockout.

My job and Mom's job, like Billy Miske's job, is to take care of you. To protect, feed, show, guide, teach, challenge, discipline, hug, help, push and raise you into good people with fulfilling lives.

You need to know how to work, fight and love like Billy. But if I could only give you one thing, it would be happiness. It makes me happy to think that you're happy. And that's enough. So this is a field guide that gives you some ideas on how to be happy.

Yesterday, I was eating fries with you on the River Congo; catching a crab with you that a sea crow dropped in our pool in Kenya; playing monsoon soccer with your tenacious face blocks in India; and "Daddy can you make me a baby pizza?" with you in Washington. Good days, under the sun.

Today is Christmas Eve, 2013. I'm far from you now,

and you've grown fast. Baby clothes get mailed off, pacifiers disappear, held hands drop, old dogs die. These things happen. We lose time, like water through our fingers, to have but not hold.

Tomorrow, Mom and I will have done what we could and you'll set out on your own. You'll meet friends and enemies. Traitors and gamblers. Hunchbacks, kings, soldiers, slaves, spies and saints. You'll get battered by storms and have your days in the sun. Great adventures await you.

Roar like Pips, and have fun.

Love,

dad

24 December 2013
Iraq

II

AWARENESSLANDIA

> Know thyself
> Know thy enemy
> A thousand battles
> A thousand victories
>
> — Sun Tzu

Do you want to be happy? If so, it helps to know:

- Where are you?
- Who are you?
- What do you want?
- What do you fear?
- Where does happiness come from?
- And how do you get it?

Where are you?

You woke into a dream. Shipwrecked on the shoals of an undiscovered country. You taste blood on your tongue. Smell sea, dirt and rain. Hear birds, wind and waves, and feel hot sun on your neck and rough coral on your palm. But you know this land like a blind man knows an elephant.

Morpheus: "The Matrix is everywhere. It is all around us. Even now, in this very room. You can see it when you look out your window or when you turn on your television. You can feel it when you go to work, when you go to church, when you pay your taxes. It is the world that has been pulled over your eyes to blind you from the truth."

Neo: "What truth?"

Morpheus: "That you are a slave, Neo. Like everyone else, you were born into bondage. Into a prison that you cannot taste or see or touch. A prison for your mind."[2]

— *The Matrix*, Wachowski & Wachowski

You slog up the beach. You stop at the frontier, facing green. Mountains and mist rise over jungle palms. Birds squawk, a branch cracks, something purrs. You smile strong and step into the Wildfar.

You were a part of Mom before you were born. You grew in her and came from her, then attached to her like a remora, only aware of your needs and her ability to meet them.

As you grew, you ventured farther from her, to your room, the house, the yard, the neighborhood, kindergarten, school, friends and beyond. Someday you'll break the pride's orbit completely and wander off to start your own prides. You're always traveling outward from your parents, a little farther each day, like stars from the big bang.

As you expand outward, so does your awareness. Every day, you learn, map, control and sense more. You carve out jungle, track pig trails, summit ridges, descend cliffs, transect canyons, cross deserts, set waypoints, mark bogs and capture territory.

You'll map and remap the jungle, until you transcend it.

Who are you?

The Leopard

Your body is like a Kid Leopard. A shell, an exoskeleton. Skin, hair, muscles and flesh. Energy, organized. It slides through the jungle and is constrained by physical laws. You are bound to it and interact with the world through it. It needs food, water, sleep. If a branch smacks you, it hurts. But if your ear gets bitten off, do you lose part of yourself? Are you less you? The body ages, dies and ends.

You aren't your body.

The Storm

Your emotions are a Storm. You have weather in your body. In your arms, legs, chest and stomach. Electricity. The same thing that makes lightning. Feel it? Hold your arms out, close your eyes and breathe in energy. Feel it flow through you? If you can't feel it, stub your toe and feel it as anger.

Sometimes the weather is nice. You're sunning on a beach like an iguana. Other times, there's a typhoon in you that wants to thrash everything.

You aren't your storm.

The Monkey

You have a Monkey in your head. Probably a chimpanzee. We all do. He's your monkey mind and he CHATTERS endlessly, "Ra, ra, ra, ra. BACOS! BACOS! BACOS!" He analyzes, judges, projects, thinks, worries, plots, calculates and schemes obsessively, recreating the world for you in your head. "I'm hungry. Throw the rock. Can I eat this? That's ugly. What if I don't make the team? Why can't you tickle yourself? That tastes bad …"

The Monkey never shuts up and hardly tires. Can you hear him in your head now? Close your eyes for a second and listen. He'll say something. He can't help it. There he is, thinking, thinking, thinking … Always.

The Monkey is a wilderness survival tool, selected into you through eons of evolution, like a muscle in your arm. He's trapped in your skull, screech-smiling and tossing books off the shelves like a maniac. As Michael Singer noted, you're living with a maniac in your head.[3]

Some people think that they're the voice in their head. Their monkey has them running around, getting as much Much as they can, making them anxious, worried, upset and neurotic. Some monkeys not only zombie-control the body they're in, but also the monkeys in other people's bodies. Your monkey is a force of great power or destruction in you. But …

You aren't your Monkey.

You're not the voice in your head. If you're the voice in your head, who is hearing it?

"The cycle of life is a struggle, and through the vortex of birth and death, I searched for the creator of this world. I never found him. Now I have found you, the creator. Your structure is dismantled. The mind has stopped creating. The delusion is destroyed."[4]

— Buddha

Identity

Your identity is who you think you are. Who you perceive and project yourself to be. Student council senators are popular, so you become a Senator. Surfers are chill cool, so you become a Surfer. Actresses are glamorous, so you become an Actress. Dishwashers don't need to study, so you become a Dishwasher. We frequently become what others love, because we need love like food.

We choose an archetype and adopt a persona from our cultural choices and think this is us. We internalize a tribe, fuse with it and re-project it.

Once, for example, a soldier returned home to the Balkans after World War II and wouldn't speak. Doctors couldn't find anything physically wrong with him, and he could read, write and follow orders. His family begged him to talk, but he wouldn't. Perplexed, doctors moved him to a veterans' hospital in another town. Thirty years later, he still hadn't spoken.

One day, a radio at the hospital happened to be broadcasting a futbol match between his hometown and their rival. At a critical moment in the game, the referee called a foul on his home team. The patient leapt from his chair and yelled, "You dumb ass! Are you trying to give them the match?" He then sat back down and never spoke again.[5]

The patient identified so strongly with his hometown futbol team that this was the only thing that incited him to speak in over 30 years, until he died.

But if this patient had been raised in his rival's hometown, would he have cheered for them? If a Pakistani imam was born in Israel, would he have become a rabbi, or vice versa? If you don't study in Soweto, can you be a dishwasher in South Africa? No. You starve. So you study.

You put your identity on like you put on a shirt. Are you a shirt?

You aren't your Identity.

Your Identity reflects you. It's part of you and what you can do. It includes your Hero and Shadow.

Your Hero

Your Hero is who you want to be and are becoming. Who you strive to be and pretend you already are. Your ideal. Your goal. King Leopard.

Your Hero is you scoring a touchdown, saying something smart, marrying a model, slaying a hyena. It's a future-focused being, fueled by want. This is the you that you project on a date or job interview. Polished, confident, perfect. You, plus 10 percent.

Your Shadow

Your Shadow is who you don't want to be and partially are. Who you strive to escape and pretend you aren't. Your anti-hero. Your fear. Crippled Leopard.

Your Shadow is you fumbling the football, saying something dumb, being rejected by a girl, running from the hyena. It's a past-focused being, fueled by fear. This is the you that you hide like a scandal. Nervous, scared, imperfect. You, minus 30 percent.

Your Identity protects you like armor. It allows you to project and hide. We fear that others will see us as we see ourselves, so we project our Hero and hide our Shadow. Sometimes, the more we project, the more we hide. The bigger a body builder's shadow becomes, the bigger he may get. Sometimes people are the opposite of what they appear.

Your Hero is mostly a good guy with positive energy who empowers you. He strives for creation, improvement and positive change. Chest out, cape flying. Look at me.

Your Shadow is mostly a destructive creature with negative energy who constrains you. He haunts you with past failures and faults. You feed your Shadow, yet you hate him, and he hates you. He is you, hating you. Never forgiving you.

The Shadow feeds on you like a parasite, eating guilt, regret and self-hate. He needs these to live. The more he eats, the stronger he becomes. To feed off you, he constantly whispers in your ear, "Why did you say that? Remember this? You should have done that …"

He whispers so quietly, just behind your ear, that you think you said it, but you didn't. He did. He constantly judges, criticizes and whips you, and replays your faults and failures over for you, like the only station on in the middle of the night in the middle of a highway in the Great American West that you can't turn off.

Your Hero and Shadow put sounds in your ears and pictures in your eyes, like an old slide projector, or a *Día de los Muertos* puppet show. Slides of future dreams and past memories, layered over the present. Sometimes your Hero is more powerful and puts more pictures; sometimes your Shadow is. They don't like each other and fight like dinosaurs, creating internal conflict.

One evening, an old Cherokee told his grandson, "My son, there is a battle between two wolves inside us all. One is Evil. It is anger, jealousy, greed, resentment, inferiority, lies and ego. The other is Good. It is joy, peace, love, hope, humility, kindness and truth."

The boy thought about this and asked, "Grandfather, which wolf wins?"

"The one you feed," the grandfather said.

Do you identify more with your Hero or Shadow? When you motivate and criticize yourself, do you use "I" or "you"? Do you, for example, say "I can beat this" or "You can beat this"? "That was stupid" or "I'm stupid"?

If you motivate yourself with "I" and criticize yourself with "you", than you possibly identify more with your Hero than your Shadow. Your Hero is dominant, and you have a generally positive view of yourself.

If you motivate yourself with "you" and criticize yourself with "I", than you possibly identify more with your Shadow. Your Shadow is dominant, and you may have a negative view of yourself.

Another way to crosscheck your self-perceived self-worth is to notice who talks more, your Hero or Shadow. Do you motivate or criticize yourself more?

As destructive as the Shadow can be, he evolved in you for a reason. He keeps your Hero from thinking he's an elephant who can fight a rhino. He has useful fear and self-discipline. If used constructively, these tools get you out of bed and to school without biting your brother on the way. Your Shadow also contains your conscience. Someday if you have kids, it'll be your job to help shape the shadows in their heads. Not too big. Not too small.

It's easy to think that you are your Monkey and Identity. A voice and an image. A picture you have of yourself. But if you are your mind, then your mind is telling itself that it is itself. Can an eye see itself? Can a knife cut itself? What do you think your mind with? Who hears the voice and sees yourself?

Something other, senses.

Your Spirit

If you aren't the Leopard, Storm, Monkey or Identity, with its Hero and Shadow, who are you? Who knows. You could be a computer program that became self-aware a second ago, complete with memories and a past. You could be a thought or trace energy. If you think a dream is real when you're in the dream, then could you be dreaming now?

Cobb: "It's only when we wake up that we realize something was actually strange. Let me ask you a question: You never really remember the beginning of a dream do you? You always wind up right in the middle of what's going on."

Ariadne: "I guess, yeah."

Cobb: "So how did we end up here?"

Ariadne: "Well, we just came from the …"

Cobb: "Think about it Ariadne, how did you get here?"[6]

— *Inception*, Christopher Nolan

How did you get here, reading this? Where did you come from? Where are you going?

None of us know where we came from before we were born or where we're going after we die. We just appear, for a while. From where? For what? We might as well just have woken up in the middle of a bikini contest. "And now, Ms. Rio de Janeiro, what do you think the meaning of life is?" Uhhh … can you repeat the question?

"If you're reading this, you've been in a coma for almost 20 years. We're trying a new technique. We don't know where this message will end up in your dream. But we hope we are getting through. Please wake up."

— Unattributed

We have to sense-guess who we are, so pick whomever you want to be. Use a strict scientific definition of man if you want. A *Homo sapien* within evolution but without pre-beginning or post-end. Use a religious idea. Any religion. Be a football player. A belly dancer. An alien. Be your Monkey if you want. Because ultimately, can anyone prove that any conception is more right than the other? Does one have to be right? To whom? You?

To your Father, who loves your Mother, saw your birth, held your hand with one finger, walked with you in the dogwoods and laugh-wrestled with you like the sun on the sea until you got too big to beat, you're infinite energy and light. Timeless. Union, perfection and happiness. Small boots by the backdoor. Red cheeks sleeping. Bone and sinew. You're the sun in the canopy, and the silence after gunfire.

You are my warrant.

"He knew only that the child was his warrant. He said: If he is not the word of God God never spoke."[7]

— Cormac McCarthy

You are Awareness.

Dad School

III

WANT & FEAR

Two significant forces batter, pull and push us, like ships in a storm: Want and Fear.

Why do you do what you do? Because you chase what you want and run from what you fear.

What do you want?

Want

Everything anyone wants is simplified in this *guía de campo* into 10 things. That is, imagine that people only want 10 things, called base commodities ("bacos"):

Physical Health: Food, water, shelter, comfort. Time and space. Things you need to survive. If you're dead, you can't catch bacos.

Security: Peace, law and order. Once alive and well, find a cave and sharpen a stick to stay that way. Protect your bacos.

Reproduction: Once alive, well and secure, replicate. Live after you die. The drive to have kids is ingrained in your cells. Evolution selected for it. Those without this urge self-select out. Biologically, you're just a survival and replication machine.[8]

Work: Labor, enterprise, production. Professional fulfillment. You want skills and work to get bacos.

Power: Power allows you to manipulate the physical and social environment to obtain more bacos. This includes justice, equality, revenge and control. How much control do you have over your environment, life and future?

Freedom: Freedom allows you to hunt bacos when and where you want.

Social Status: Do you want people to like you? Do you want respect? If you're in a tribe, then you're not alone in the rift valley. If you're alone, you can be eaten (dead) and can't replicate (future dead).

Emotional Health: Does somebody love you? Do you love yourself? Do you want human contact, attention and affection?

Intellectual Health: Mental stimulation. Intelligence, clarity, creativity, innovation and adventure.

Spiritual Health: Mission, meaning, morals, ideology and purpose. Why are you here? What are you doing?

Bacos are physical commodities like nutrients and nonphysical commodities like power. Physical bacos exist in objects, and nonphysical bacos exist in thoughts. People produce, acquire and trade bacos. They trade them directly and indirectly via goods, services, currency and ideas. People make economic calculations to trade bacos even when bacos, such as social status, are difficult to quantify and monetize. As such, economic concepts apply to baco transactions.

Life is a running series of energy transactions. If you make (Work) five spears (Security) but only need four, you can trade one for a book (Intellectual Health). A soldier risks Physical Health for meaning (Spiritual Health). A fugitive risks Physical Health for Freedom. A wire-walker trades Security for Social Status. Yoda traded companionship (Emotional Health) for Spiritual Health on Dagobah.

Money is a liquid form of bacos. It represents bacos so they can be traded easier. It's a currency. A means to an end, not an end. Not a baco. Why do you want money? For the paper it's on? To buy a car? Why do you want a car? For freedom and social status?

Go to the core of what you and others want to determine motive. Determine motive to predict action.

Fear

What do you fear?

Baco loss.

Want pulls you. Fear drives you. They are similar replicates. With want, you spend physical and mental energy to obtain bacos. With fear, you spend energy not to lose them. Losing bacos causes pain.

The fear of losing bacos motivates more than the chance to acquire bacos.[9] Studies, for example, show that people dislike losing $1,000 more than they like gaining $1,000. This is called loss aversion.[10]

You thus, for example, have a certain amount of physical health. You want a certain amount more and you have a certain amount of fear of losing each unit. How much physical health you want and how much you fear losing it depends on how valuable physical health is to you, which is influenced by how much you have. This can be visualized like:

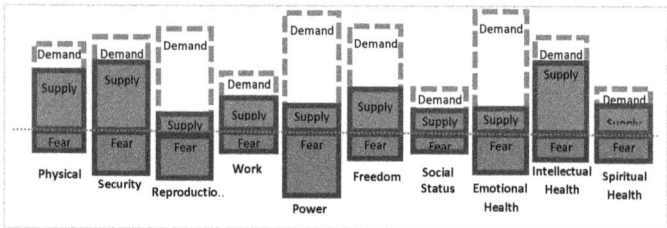

IV

THE HAPPY HUNT

How do you get happy?

By anticipating and getting bacos. When you do, your body releases chemicals, like dopamine (for anticipating) and opioids (for getting). These make you feel good. You like feeling good, so you try to get and keep as many bacos as possible. This process motivates (rewards and punishes) you with pleasure and pain, so you repeat it, ad infinitum.[11,12,13,14,15]

Evolution has biologically engineered, or chemically incentivized you to take actions that maximize utility and minimize pain by providing opioid hits from acquiring as many baco units as possible, as cheaply as possible, over time. That is, you acquire bacos to acquire opioids to acquire utility and avoid pain, in order to increase evolutionary fitness. This is a biological program, physically hardwired into us by evolution. Biologically, the goal is to catch and keep as many bacos as you can.

It's like a drug deal. You hunt bacos and give them to a drug-dealing Narco in your head, who gives you opioid hits for them.[16]

Where do you get bacos from?

From objects and thoughts.

Objects, like food, can contain intrinsic physical bacos. You're hungry, you eat a burger, the nutrients interact with your body to increase physical health, you satisfy the hunger, your body releases opioids and you're happy.

This makes sense. An external physical input causes a physiological chemical reaction in your body that satisfies a physical desire and releases opioids that produce happiness. What's strange, however, is that thoughts can do the same thing.

Thoughts, like the idea of food, can contain extrinsic mental bacos. What if you're starving in the Sahara and someone tells you that they have a cheeseburger for you. You're going to live. You're happy. You haven't eaten the burger, and nothing physical has entered your body, yet your mouth waters and you're happy. Why? Because the thought satisfies a mental desire, which causes a chemical reaction that releases chemicals that produce happiness.

Likewise, what happens if you recall a joke, remember a funny movie or think about an upcoming vacation? You're happy. What happens if your teacher tells you that you have to give a speech to your class in five minutes on Jamestown? You're nervous.

Studies show that imagined pleasure is pleasurable, and imagined pain is painful.[17] Thus:

A thought, alone, can make you happy. Or unhappy.

"The best part about doing cocaine, is going to get the cocaine."

— Adam Carolla

Thoughts can cause physiological chemical reactions, because sometimes the mind can't tell the difference between a physical hyena on the plain and a mental hyena in a dream. To the mind, both physical objects and mental thoughts can be real.

"Everything you can imagine is real."

— Pablo Picasso

Objects can contain intrinsic and extrinsic bacos, and thoughts can contain extrinsic bacos. We consume these physically and mentally. We eat thoughts like food. Positive thoughts taste like cake. Negative thoughts taste like a cow tongue sandwich. We know and experience this. Yet frequently we cling to negative thoughts and go on and on, chewing cow tongue sandwiches.

Baco-loading

Objects and thoughts contain extrinsic bacos because we put them there. We load ideas into them like we stuff a turkey. A dollar, for example, is only worth a dollar if we think it is. Otherwise, it's just a piece of paper. A diamond only has power and social status because we stuff it with power and social status. Otherwise, it's just a rock.

The burger contains physical nutrients, and the diamond contains the idea of social status. Both, however, are real to the mind, and the Narco releases opioids for them. To the mind, it's as if the diamond contains an actual physical protein called social status.

Obtaining happiness from objects that you load with extrinsic happiness is sometimes like throwing tacos down a well, then figuring out how to get the tacos out of the well to eat them and worrying as you do. You already had the tacos to begin with.

The Ideosphere

Since thoughts can be as real to your mind as a hyena, your mind thinks that they exist outside you like a hyena. But, they are created and exist inside you.

We baco-load objects and lay an array of ideas over the physical world like a GPS layer: "A diamond is valuable. A bike provides freedom. Student council senators are cool. Mason is popular."

We set conditions for happiness in different areas of our lives, then try to meet them: "If I get a bike, I'll be happy. If I get elected to student council, I'll be cool, so I'll be happy. If Mason likes me, I'll be desired, so I'll be happy."

Our Monkey and consciousness spend considerable time and energy every day bouncing back and forth between the ideas in this ideosphere we make and maintain to worry about them: "How can I get a bike? How can I get elected? How can I get Mason to like me?"

When we satisfy these conditions and get something, we set new conditions, farther out. We're biologically hardwired to do this. To strive and survive. Those who didn't died.

We have our head in the clouds and can live in our mental world more than in the physical world. How many times today did you consciously watch and experience something physical, in the present, for its own sake, without layering it with thought or judgment? What percentage of your day was spent in ideas (like this one)?

> "If the doors of perception were cleansed, everything would appear to man as it is, infinite. For man has closed himself up, till he sees all things thro' narrow chinks of his cavern."[18]

> — William Blake[19]

Sometimes, an idea cloud becomes a thought pit. It entraps and sickens us, and we live in the bottom of its gravitational well. "I can't believe Mason broke up with me. How can I get him back? How can I get him back? How can I get him back? …"

What, for example, was the last major problem you had? Did anyone else have this problem? Did they occupy the same mental geography as you, and truly care about what happened to you or how you felt? Probably not, because they were attached to their own problems. Chances are, it was just you and your problem, living together like cellmates.

Thus, we get objects and thoughts that contain bacos, we give these to our brain, our brain gives us opioids for them and we're happy (Addendum A). This happiness process has three consequences:

1) The fact that you have to get something to get opioids from yourself, and can't simply access and enjoy the opioids that you produce makes you an open system, which cleaves the mind from the body and creates awareness.[20]

2) Since you baco-load happiness into objects, you determine how many obstacles you put between yourself and happiness, which can prevent you

from being happy - or free you to be happy. You build the prison, so you have the keys to it.

3) The fact that thoughts can physiologically make you happy or sad is the escape hatch in the happy hunt. You don't control your fundamental base chemistry, but you do control thoughts, and this loophole creates an opportunity to increase happiness - and a pitfall to produce sadness.

In Sum

Our bodies crave, our emotions roll and thunder, our Monkey worries, schemes, analyzes and teeth-chatters, our Identity and self-worth carbon-fuse, our Hero boasts and projects, and our Shadow critiques and surfaces while we obsessively chase Leopard King Want and run from Hyena Fear to get and protect bacos for opioid hits from ourselves.

Every day.

All the time.

Over and over again.

And this is just inside your skull. Outside, you're reacting to input in a fluid landscape, full of collaborators and thieves, with similar mental-emotional hurricanes and confrontational force vectors.

This is your normal, balanced state.

Given this, most people are out of control. We're reactionary and neurotic. We don't know why we do the things we do. We make decisions and justify reasons for them afterward. We then expend considerable money, effort, time and energy to create peace gaps and take vacations from ourselves. Michael Singer once said something to the effect that; A true five-minute vacation from yourself in your office could be more relaxing than a five-day vacation with yourself in the Yucatan.

But!

You can manage and optimize several steps in the process that produces happiness to increase happiness. You can balance the body and leash the Monkey. We can do this by:

- Targeting

- Hunting

- Healing and

- Managing

Dad School

V

TARGET

What makes you happy, and what can you do to get it?

If you don't have goals to maximize happiness over time, you'll blindly follow urges for immediate gratification from one want island to the next. People spend lives hunting the wrong things, trying to get things they think they want or things the Monkey, Fear, insecurity, anger or other people eat. They're lost before they've begun.

If you won the lottery, what would you do? If, after you bought a car and took a vacation you'd still roughly be doing what you're doing now (like building houses, running a company, making music, helping others, raising kids …), you're aligned. That said, sometimes you have to serve your country, feed your family and make sacrifices.

Do whatever makes you happy that doesn't hurt someone. But cross-check it to see if something else can make you more happy over time. Why do you want to be a _____? For power? Why do you need power? Are you trying to fill a hole? Can you heal the hole instead of feed it, and generate more positive impact and constructive happiness elsewhere?

To optimize happiness over time, identify your wants and fears, refine your goals to satisfy your wants, and prioritize your limited time and energy to achieve these.

Identify

What do you want, why do you want it and what will feed it? How much Security, Reproduction, Work, Power, Freedom, Social Status and Physical, Emotional, Intellectual and Spiritual Health do you want? Simplify your wants into these 10 categories. Everybody wants something.

"Nobody in this world feels whole or complete. We all sense some gap in our character, something we need or want but cannot get on our own. ... Look at people ... focusing on the gaps ... that is the raw material of seduction."[21]

— Robert Greene

Be honest with yourself. Everyone is telling themselves a story - about who they are and what they're doing. Almost everyone is the hero of their story, even bad guys, and we use fig leaves to justify darker desires. What's your story? What do you really want?

What fears drive you? Are they rational? Danger is external. Fear is internal. You create your own agony.

"Fear is not real. The only place that fear can exist is in our thoughts of the future. It is a product of our imagination, causing us to fear things that do not at present and may not ever exist. This is near insanity, Kitai. Do not misunderstand me: Danger is very real, but fear is a choice."[22]

— *After Earth*, Whitta and M. Night Shyamalan

Fear creates a force vector that can push you toward unnecessary objectives. Are the fears that drive you sensible? Are you, for example, trying to be the smartest, bravest, strongest or fastest _____, because you're afraid nobody will remember you if you're not? Will anyone remember you two hundred years from now? Your dog, Don Macho, pees all over town, probably thinking he's accomplishing a lot.

Set, Refine, Reset

Once you know what you want, what can you do to get it? Intelligent people don't get all A's and go to Yale; they arrange the world to get what they want. But getting all A's and going to Yale can help do this.

First, make a want list. In one column, list the goals and projects you're working on right now, like getting all A's, being the starting running back, writing a field guide, plotting revenge. In another column, list why you want these things. What motivates you to get out of bed, get to school and get them? What bacos does each goal give you if you accomplish it?

Are the bacos that your goals produce the same as the bacos you really want? If, for example, helping animals makes you happy, why are you becoming an accountant? Life throws you off-balance, which is good. This is how you grow. But people get sidetracked. Are you doing what makes you happy over time?

Continually reassess your goals to meet your wants to optimize happiness over time. Also:

1) Avoid doing long-term, energy-intensive projects just for money. Before starting a large project, ask

yourself, "If this fails completely and I lose all my money on it, will I still have loved doing it, and will I have made something meaningful?"

2) Everyone has a thing. This is what they do when they're not working like hiking, hunting, running, sailing, surfing, knitting, heroin. What's your thing? Make it constructive. Better yet, make it what you do when you're working. Get one of those "get rich snorting heroin between your toes" jobs.

3) When the director of the Grant Study, which has tracked 268 men for 72 years, was asked what he has learned from the study of this many men for this long, he said, "The only thing that really matters in life is your relationships to other people."[23]

4) Drop negative, destructive goals. Is the core intent of your goals positive and constructive, or negative and destructive? Are you building or destroying something? If your original intent is positive your product will be. Destructive goals generate unhappiness in negative feedback loops. If you set out to hurt someone, you'll hurt yourself too.

"Before you embark on a journey of revenge, dig two graves."

— Confucius

5) Create positive impact.

Prioritize

Once you've set your goals, prioritize them. Break them

into A, B and C tiers. A's are like graduating with all A's. C's are like organizing your playlist. Are you spending so much time cleaning your hotel room at the Sahara that you can't leave for work? Next week, will you wish you had cleaned your vents or finished your statistics?

Do A's. Drop C's. Advance. Most C's will take care of themselves, or become A's to complete. This will optimally allocate your limited time and energy to the right targets to maximize happiness over time. This is pretty simple, but a lot of people don't get this far.

In Sum

You're blessed if you can do what you want. Sometimes you can't. You do what you have to do. You chop cane to put your son through school. But there's happiness in this, too. Maybe more. Simplify your life. Distill it to white bone. To creation, sun, salt and family.

If you navigate the shopping cart, it shouldn't lose a wheel and crash into a crack house. Nobody sets out to be an executioner, Jungler or crackhead, yet there are executioners, Junglers and crackheads. What happened? If you wake up one day in the middle of torturing someone, put the heretic's fork down, pick up your go bag, go straight to Ulaanbaatar and start over. Any moment you want to go to Ulaanbaatar, you can.

Lastly, take chances when young. Especially when broke. Broke makes it great and enriches you when old. Hunt big. Run far. Ride hard, wet, weathered and beat, with gut and grit over tundra and trail, because it's hard to be reckless and brave when old, and time is the only commodity you can't get more of.

Dad School

VI

HUNT

Learning one of the best ways to learn. Udaipur, India.

The most evident way to increase happiness is to comply like a convict with the opioid drug deal and try to get as much Much as you can for the Narco. Get bacos for opioid hits. Play along. This is what most people do all day every day until death do they part.

Hunting bacos produces happiness but does not maximize it. It has limitations and collateral damage. But we have to do it. You need food, water and shelter. Satisfying base needs like these frees you to experience deeper fulfillment. Mastering the rat race frees you to transcend it.

The hunt is also fun. How is it that our lives become so compromised, parceled, hedged and halved that part of us longs to crash in the Congo, transect the Empty Quarter and shipwreck on a deserted island, to watch everything we've built burn to the ground, so that we can escape a soft body in a square cubical and harden, scar and test ourselves like our ancestors on the open plain?

Here are some hard skills to hunt bacos and manage external circumstances to increase internal happiness. Use them to get in the game and get bacos. Get hit, get slammed, get up and get things. You're an active participant in physical life, and this generates movement, innovation, change, challenge and growth.

Responsibility

First, it's not your parents', your spouse's, your friends', your maid's, your video games' or your government's responsibility to entertain and take care of you. It's not their job to make you happy. It's yours. And they don't make you unhappy. You do.

Focus

A lot of success and happiness in life simply depends on what you focus on — what you turn your head to look at.

Once, in high school, I threw an interception. An out route. The DB ran it in for a touchdown. Next series, I did the same thing. Two interceptions, two touchdowns. Next series, all I could think was, "Don't throw an interception." I started visualizing interceptions instead of completions. Failure, instead of success.

That game, I threw four touchdowns — for the other team. Four interceptions, four touchdowns. I didn't throw any touchdowns for our team. That's hard to do. It probably set a school record. My focus predetermined my outcome. Visualize touchdowns.

Focus on the positive. The hunt will be cold and difficult, but the challenge and outcome are worth it.

Focus on the results you want. Those who focus on the pain, quit. Those who focus on the result, win.

Focus on the hunt. Take one step at a time. Breathe, then operate. Hyperventilating won't help, and there's only so much you can do. If the op fails after this, it fails.

Once, a free safety had 26 tackles in his first college game as a starter. It's unusual for a safety to have this many tackles, and it tied a school record.

The next Monday after practice, his coach called him into his office. The safety thought he was going to get praised for playing so well. Instead, his coach yelled at him.

"You better not frickin think," the coach growled, "that you're going to go out there every week and try to break some kind of school record."

"Coach," the safety replied, "I didn't even know there was a record. I was just trying to kill the ball carrier."

Kill the ball carrier, and the rest will take care of itself.

Mindset

Your perception and attitude impact your performance

and output. Try this. Do 55 burpees in a row, two different ways:

A) Working down: Do 10 burpees, counting up to 10. Then do 9 burpees, counting up to 9. Then do 8 burpees, counting up to 8. Repeat until you're at 0. That's 55 burpees total, working down from 10 to 0.

B) Working up: Do the same thing in reverse. Do 1 burpee, then return to 0. Do 2 burpees, then return to 0. Do 3 burpees, and repeat until you're at 10.

Both ways, you do 55 burpees. Mentally, however, tactic A appears to start hard and get easier as you go, while tactic B appears to start easy and get harder as you go. Objectively, you do the same amount of work both ways, but subjectively, which seems easier?

There's no right answer, because perception is relative to the observer. But the easier something seems to individuals, the better they perform, and you can frequently see the same objective several ways. Mentally, you can make the same objective easy or hard. How does running a six-minute mile tomorrow at dawn sound? Fast? How does it sound if a hyena is chasing you? Not fast enough.

Assess a difficult objective and choose the most productive mental route to assault it.

Get your gun right.

Get your mind right.

Get going.

Beat your Opponent With Preparation and Discipline

"Every battle is won before it is fought."

— Sun Tzu

The game is won in the off-season, when you get off the couch and your opponent doesn't. Every time you stay on the couch, pull up short, take a rest or cut a corner, you make it easier for the hyenas to catch you.

"If you want to be the best, you have to do things that other people aren't willing to do."

— Michael Phelps

Work Hard Now or Work Harder Later

What's easier: forcing yourself to get good grades now, or slacking off and working in the Dakar sewer later? Either way, you're going to have to work hard. Tomorrow, what will you wish you had done today?

"The more you sweat in peace, the less you bleed in war."

— Attributed to Sun Tzu

Run as far as you possibly can and stop. You can run 20 percent farther. You can run a mile on a peanut. Your legs don't give out; your head does.

Procrastination is a friend or foe. He tempts the weak. He hands out naps before every race. The weak drift into his warm roadside tavern and wake up with a 25-pound plate on their chest. If you're tough, Procrastination is an ally who culls your competition.

"I hated every minute of training, but I said, 'Don't quit. Suffer now and live the rest of your life as a champion.'"

— Muhammad Ali

Hard Helps

Both procrastination and hard eliminate competition to create opportunity.

Once, two men were walking through the bush when they came upon a hungry lion. The lion looked up at them, about to spring.

"Run," one guy whispered.

"Why?" The other asked. "The lion can catch us."

"I don't have to outrun the lion. I just have to outrun you."

Everyone could say they're Army Rangers, but then it would be meaningless to be a Ranger. Being a Ranger would be like being a person. You have to survive selection.

If it doesn't get hard, others won't quit. If others don't quit, you can't distinguish yourself. If you want to distinguish yourself, seek hard. Lean into the rain while others cower from it. You're going to get wet anyway. You'll dry. And when you do, you'll hold something they don't.

"It's hard to beat someone who doesn't quit."

— Babe Ruth

As said, Lord Shiva doesn't give you what you want. He gives you what you need. Pain teaches.

"A smooth sea never made a skillful sailor."

— English Proverb

Start. Grind. Margin.

If you do 100 burpees in a row, which is the hardest? The hundredth? No. The hundredth is one of the easiest, if not the easiest one. Why? Cause 90 percent of doing something is done in your head.

The first burpee is one of the hardest. Fifty percent of doing something is starting it. Showing up on time with a good attitude will get you a lot further in life than it should.

Burpees 2 to 20 aren't bad. Your body is fresh and your mind strong. Burpees 30 to 40 are frequently some of the toughest, because you're physically tired and mentally know that you still have 70 to go.

It gets easier around 40, because your mind accepts the new reality instead of fighting it.

Burpees 40 to 90 are the grind. Maintenance. Keeping your head above water. Good enough to not lose ground today.

The last 10 burpees are the margin. They pay the

biggest dividends. Most people quit during the grind, or at the end of it, when "good enough" ends and uncomfortable begins. Get into the margin for exponential gains.

How You Feel about it Doesn't Matter

Feelings matter, but not to burpees. Not to the mission. Not to anyone but you and your family. Nobody cares how you feel. Life doesn't. Selection doesn't. Either you do it or don't.

If something is hard, have you tried complaining about it? Is the story you're telling yourself helping you get what you want? If not, you won't get it.

"If you think you can do a thing or you think you can't do a thing, you're right."

— Henry Ford

The only way Through It Is Through It

If you want to have done 200 burpees, you have to do 200 burpees. You can't do 500 burpees in a row, but you can always do one more.

Pain Is Progress

As said, pain is inevitable, but suffering is optional. Turn on pain, accept it and breathe through it. Trying to avoid unavoidable pain makes it more painful, and the more you suffer now, the better you feel later — if you cash in the investment and enjoy the dividend.

"Ask yourself, 'Can I give more?' The answer is usually yes."

— Paul Tergat, Kenyan Marathoner

When Mom birthed Boo in Georgetown, she was lying on a gurney. She had been laboring for 24 hours, but Boo was inverted in the belly, so the doctors decided to do a cesarean. They numbed her and sliced her stomach open. She lay there, calm and conscious with makeup on, talking while latex gloves slide in her like a sci-fi film, digging to turn and extract Boo. They pulled on her ribs and moved organs. Her stomach was open but she wasn't in any significant pain. She was conscious and coherent, talking like normal.

It was then that a thought occurred to me; pain is not real. Or, pain is not real until it is made real by the mind. Until then, it's just neurons. Signals. Energy, unrealized. It's something that can be blocked, overcome, defeated and lived with, to the point that someone can chat while their stomach is gashed.

How much pain can be disregarded because the brain overreacts to pain signals? If whatever causes the pain won't cause lasting cellular damage, manage it.

Once, when I was 11, your uncle and I carried a boulder out to the middle of a frozen pond in Michigan. We lifted it as high as we could and threw it as far as we could. It smacked the ice at our feet. The ice CRACKED and GROANED, deep and long, like rolling thunder under our feet. It was horrifying and beautiful. And dumb. We caught our breath, yelled and ran off the pond.

There are some memorable sounds like this. The CRACK of a bat on a ball, a SWOSH, WIND in cottonwoods, ECHOS in canyons, waves in Mombasa, THUNDER in Tsavo. There's rain on your bedroom window, and snow falling deathly silent on snow. But this is the best, and I've heard it four times: The sound of your baby coming from nothing into something, from God knows where, crying so real and alive for the first time.

Work Hard, Work Smart

What rooms do you spend most of your day in? Can you walk into them and say, "I can outwork anyone in this room"? If not, you're probably not working hard enough. If so, good, but you're not in the right room. Say and do this until you end up in a room where you're not sure you can outwork everyone in it. That's the room you want to be in. Until you transcend it.

If you have a choice between taking an easy road or a hard road, the hard road is usually the right one. But not always.

You can outwork almost anyone, which will pass almost everyone, but to beat the last 5 percent, if that's your goal, you have to work smart too, because they're working as hard as you.

One day, my high school physics teacher started pushing on a wall in class. He pushed hard for a minute, asking, "Is this work?" It sure looked like it. He kept pushing and asked, "Is this work?" I finally said yes.

"Why?" The professor asked.

"Because you're tired," I replied.

"It's not," he said, "because the wall isn't moving!"

In physics, the definition of work is:

Work = Force x Displacement x Cosine(theta)

That is, for work to happen, something must MOVE.

Don't push on walls.

Think Smart

Working smart can mean thinking differently — innovating and seeing opportunities others don't.

"Talent hits a target no one else can hit. Genius hits a target no one else can see."[24]

— Arthur Schopenhauer

Think about different ways to think. Notice when you're transmitting, observing and receiving.

Transmitting: While transmitting, you're consciousness links with your Monkey and you see the world through his eyes, filtered with ideas and layered with constructs. Your Monkey and consciousness proactively crank at problem sets and project thoughts. You assess, resolve and advance, trying to control situations and outcomes. You're caffeinated and active, talking instead of listening, or politely waiting to talk.

Observing: While observing, your consciousness steps away from the Monkey while he continues iterating. You observe the Raw World As Is Now (RWAIN) without (much) thinking, loading or judging, and your awareness shifts to the present.

Receiving: While receiving, your consciousness passively observes images and ideas surfacing from your subconscious. You surrender control, wander far and wide, and watch random, broken ideas aimlessly flicker and go, unharnessed. You're listening and receptive. You can consciously slip into this mode as you fall asleep. When you lay down to sleep, for example, sometimes you're still transmitting and pushing out thoughts like, "I should have said _____. I can't believe _____ ..." As you transition to sleep, you stop doing this and start receiving images, which transition to dreams. Try to observe this next time you sleep. If you can't sleep, it might be because you can't stop transmitting.

Normally, we operate in transmit. Transmit gets us across the street without getting hit. Driving, going to school and working all require transmit. In transmit, have your Monkey use thought patterns instead of just bouncing around, like: linear, opposite, lateral, parody, irony, assumptions, stories, what if?, creative ...

Strength

Somewhere at some point when you're not expecting it, life will hit you in the back of the knees with a bat, because Zeus doesn't think your plans are as important as you do. What are you going to do?

It's the Little Things that Count

Wash borrowed trucks. Send thank you cards. Buy someone a Coke. Listen. Run two steps farther than the finish line.

I'm Bad at Math

"You're right. You don't ever study."[25]

— Eric Thomas

Fail

Don't fear failure. Failure forces innovation. It gives you the opportunity to adapt, improvise and overcome — to make something better. When you're done with a screenplay, you're halfway done.

The strong embrace their weaknesses and mistakes. Is it better to externalize and laugh at your mistakes, or internalize and hide them? Holding negative energy in, instead of letting it flow through you, feeds the Shadow.

As said, bad news doesn't get better with time, and the cover-up is worse than the crime. Admit your mistakes, take the pain and move on. The faster you do this, the faster you advance. You can't surpass your mistakes until you embrace them, because pain doesn't leave until it teaches us what we need to know.

"You were born to make mistakes, not fake perfection."

— Unattributed

Failure, like pain, teaches. Once, at the beginning of a security course, they told us to always lock our doors, and if someone ever pulls up alongside us and aims a gun at us while we're driving, to brake, even though your instinct is to accelerate. I understood clearly, academically.

A week later, I forgot to lock my door during a night exercise, which had nothing to do with locking your doors. During the exercise, I stopped at a suspicious makeshift roadblock on a small road in the dark forest. Two heavily armed insurgents in unmarked camos and balaclavas emerged from the night and approached through my headlights. As they did, a BANG exploded in the woods to my right. I jumped in my seat and snapped right. When I did, a guerilla snuck up from behind my left shoulder and ripped my driver side door open. He grabbed the wheel and I hit the gas. I escaped, but failed the exercise.

A few days later in another exercise, two guys on a motorcycle sped up alongside me as I was driving. The guy in back drew a gun on me. When this happens, your adrenaline shoots and you instinctively floor it. Which, counterintuitively, is the exact wrong move. If you can't ram or run them over (a car is a 2,000 pound weapon), slam your breaks. I floored it, and gave him an easy kill shot to the back of my spine.

But I've never forgotten those lessons. And I can't remember the ones I half-guessed right the first time.

Successful people get knocked down and get back up. Others don't. Successful people actually get knocked down more than unsuccessful people, because they keep getting back up for more.

Once, Kidogo was playing his first year of football as an Ankle Biter. He was one of the youngest and smallest kids on the team. One practice, an older and bigger center kept pummeling him all practice, since he was playing nose guard on the scout team. Finally, Kidogo had enough and got mad. He exploded off the line and surged back into the guy. The guy knocked him down again, but Kidogo got up, lined up and went at him again. The guy knocked Kidogo down every play, but Kidogo kept getting up and coming back for more. Boo wrote a story that mentioned this and said Kidigo "was known for how aggressive he was standing by his friend's side." I was proud of you.

Sometimes, the point isn't to "win," but to get up. If you're not failing, you're not pushing yourself hard enough. Challenge yourself and push your comfort zone. You can't grow otherwise.

And failure frequently isn't failure. When a setback occurs, look around and say, "Okay, that stinks. But where is the opportunity and happiness here?" Sometimes all you'll see is more setbacks. Just keep looking, because if all you can see is opportunity and happiness, you'll find them, by definition.

One day a farmer's donkey fell into a well. The animal cried for hours as the farmer tried to figure out what to do. Finally, he decided that the animal was old, and the well needed to be covered up anyway. It wasn't worth it to try to retrieve the donkey.

So the farmer grabbed a shovel and started tossing dirt into the well. The donkey realized what was happening and cried horribly. Then, after a few minutes, he quieted down.

A few shovel loads later, the farmer looked down into the well. He smiled at what he saw. With each shovelful of dirt that hit the donkey's back, the donkey would shake it off and step up.

The farmer kept shoveling dirt on the donkey. Each time, the punda stepped up. He did this until he stepped over the well's edge, shook himself off and trotted home.

Perfection

Don't worry, everyone is winging it. Just do your best.

"The only normal people are the ones we don't know well enough."

— Alfred Adler

Deconstructing Threats

People will want what you have, and sometimes you have to protect it. Threats are real and mortal. Look at the hyena. Look at the snake. Why is the chameleon camouflaged?

There are, for example, hives within hives of terrorists out there, despite all we've imprisoned and killed. They're hidden in cities, villages, houses and families like a virus, boiling hate and sharpening knives. There are entire swaths of earth where people will cut your throat like a goat if they get their hands on it. Just because you're an American, a Hindu, a Yazidi, whatever. It's just hate, either way. Hate and evil. This is not an exaggeration. This is just how it is.

The knives will come out, as they have for eons, for the road to your warm home is bathed in blood and bones.

One day a scorpion was walking along a riverbank, trying to find a way across the river. After a little while, he came across a frog.

"Will you give me a ride across the river?" Scorpion asked.

"No," Frog quickly replied.

"Why not?"

"Because, Mr. Scorpion, if I put you on my back and give you a ride, you will sting me and I will drown."

"But if I sting you, Mr. Frog," said Scorpion, "and you drown, then I will drown, too."

Frog thought about this a minute, then said, "I guess you're right. Okay, I will give you a ride."

Scorpion climbed on Frog's back, and they started across the river.

Halfway across the river, Frog felt a sharp pain in his back. He looked back and saw that Scorpion had stung him.

Frog started to panic as the venom raced through him and he became paralyzed. As he drew his last breath and began to sink, he said, "But Scorpion! Why did you sting me? Now we will both drown!"

"I could not help it," Scorpion replied. "It's in my nature."

To counter threats, see motive.

Sit and watch people in a public area, like a park. Interestingly, you get them. You can tell where they came from, what they're doing and where they're going. There's a student studying. A lawyer late to a meeting. A widow strolling. Parents trying to relax on a relaxing vacation. A laborer scratching lottery cards, hoping to change his life.

Anyone who looks out of place probably is. That's why good cover stories are visual, and covert acts are hidden within legitimate ones. The second you have to explain a cover story, you appear as guilty as you are.

You can do the same thing with people's accessories, cars and houses. What do a digital watch, a nose ring, pearls, cigarettes, a lacrosse stick, a bike rack, an orange car, a messy car, exotic statues or a drum set suggest? What's on your date's shelves and in their closet?

You can accurately infer a significant amount about someone from a three-second glance, and even more from a short conversation, if you're looking and listening. People are constantly, inadvertently signaling what they want, fear and lack, despite their laborious and exhausting efforts to camouflage themselves by projecting their Hero and hiding their Shadow. You can almost see people driving along force vectors, chasing Want and fleeing Fear.

Intent is obvious. And the older you get, the more obvious it becomes.

Find motive, in yourself and others. Why is this guy buying me drinks? Why am I getting a face tattoo?

Determine what people want and fear. Which bacos are they chasing? There are only 10. Don't overcomplicate it. Does a politician want power? Does a monk want enlightenment? People want various combinations of them all, but they're usually focused on one or two, and their focus dictates their actions, which predicts their behavior. You won't always be right, but you'll be right enough.

If you can roughly identify what someone wants and fears, you may know them better than they know themselves. People aren't as complicated as they think they are.

Building Consensus

To build consensus, show people how they can get what they want by buying what you're selling. Appeal to their most carnal wants, because these are the most forceful. It's about them and what they want, not you. Give them what they want to get what you want.

Compliment and empower people. Winston Churchill once said something like; if you want someone to have a certain quality, impute it on them.

If you tell someone, for example, "It's refreshing working with you, because you're always on time," they'll try to always be on time. They'll strive to live up to the positive image you've painted of them. Paint this in front of a group and they'll try even harder.

Once, when I was 12, I was whining about being sick. Grammy said, "Ya, you must really be sick, because you never complain." I thought, "I complain all the time. Damn, now I can't whine about being sick." When complaining, you don't have to be right or make sense, that's what's so great about it.

Compliments motivate more than complaints, yet people criticize more than they compliment. The man above compliments. The man below criticizes. Try to compliment or highlight someone's effort every day.

People try and work hard, and are rarely recognized. When was the last time someone told you that you did a good job? The more leverage and power you acquire, the more people you can help and empower. The more people you care for, the greater you are. Leverage, leverage, leverage. Financial and social leverage.

Set tone. Decide what's right and do it. Then, others will follow.

"A good man draws a circle around himself and cares for those within it: his woman, his children. Other men draw a large circle and bring within it their brothers and sisters. But some men have a great destiny. They must draw around themselves a circle that includes many, many more."[26]

— *10,000 B.C.*, Emmerich & Kloser

Conquer

Crush weakness. To do something hard, use Want and Fear. Use your Monkey. That's what he's there for. Either you use him or he uses you.

First, put a simple picture of what you want in your head. A hero pic. The goal. If you want to be a commando, picture yourself rigged. If you want to be an astronaut, picture yourself standing on the moon like Neil Armstrong. One picture. Focus on that like the North Star.

The picture has to be simple, because near your perceived limit, you will only feel pain, and pain vaporizes complexity. It kills logic, half-hearted intent and the story you've told others and yourself. You won't think straight because you won't think. You'll only feel. Feel like quitting. Some people seek pain precisely so they can escape their Monkey and don't have to think.

Pain vaporizes your big plan logic and tries to replace it with poisonous thoughts: "Well, I got further than most. … I'm too young for this. … There's still two more weeks of this. … I'll regroup and try later. … I have a medical excuse. …"

> "It isn't the mountains ahead to climb that wear you
> down; it's the pebble in your shoe."

> — Muhammed Ali

Block excuses and refocus on your hero pic. Stay on
your pic. It'll get you where you want to go. Don't let your
monkey mind wander. Again, life is what you look at.
That's it. It's not hard. Look at your Hero.

Would you rather have temporary pain and permanent
victory, or temporary relief and permanent failure? Cause
those are your choices, and "we are the choices we
make."[27]

Focus on your hero pic, not the finish line. They're
different. The finish line is an artificial limit against which
you scale perceived ability. It's also a weight. When you're
dead tired, instead of thinking about how far you still have
to go, just think about running to the next telephone pole.
Take victory in pieces.

Positive thoughts are better than negative thoughts,
because negative thoughts can have collateral damage and
downstream repercussions, so try to motivate yourself and
others with positive energy. But since fear motivates more
than want, and sometimes you gotta get angry.

> "You can tell the greatness of a man by what makes
> him angry."

> — Abraham Lincoln

So make a fail pic. Again, a simple pic. Consolidate
what you're afraid of into one pic. The thing you want

least opposite the thing you want most. That which you fear. Picture yourself coming home and telling your buddies that you quit, selling a flaccid excuse to hide the fact that you weren't good, clever or tough enough.

Doing this cages and controls your fear, instead of letting it run wild and control you. You're also turning on it and using it to create something constructive. The energy is there anyway, so redirect, release and use it. It's just energy, which can change form.

"If you don't hunt it down and kill it, it will hunt you down and kill you."[28]

— Flannery O'Connor

Self-motivate. People who succeed, succeed when nobody is looking, because when nobody is looking, they are. What you do when nobody is looking is more important than what you do when they are, because this reveals what kind of person you are.

The Journey Is the Destination

Imagine having everything you could ever want in one room. Food, candy, toys, friends, security, love, etc. Anytime you wanted something, you just had to pick it up. Would you be happy?

"Men are happiest chasing something they can't quit catch."

— Unattributed

Hunting is fun.

Getting bacos can make you feel better. Sleeping in a warm bed usually feels better than sleeping in the cold rain (unless the warm bed is in prison), but getting things leaves us desirous and rarely satisfied. As soon as you get something, the Monkey wants more.

Hunting is autotelic. Its purpose is partially the point. Enjoy the hunt as much as the kill, for the obstacle is the path, and there's meaning in it.

"There is no way to happiness. Happiness is the way."

— Unattributed

One day a traveler walking along a lane came upon three stonecutters working in a quarry. Each was cutting a block of stone. Interested to find out what they were working on, he asked the first stonecutter what he was doing.

"I'm cutting a stone," the stonecutter said. "It's miserable, but it's a living."

No wiser, the traveler walked to the second stonecutter and asked him what he was doing. He appeared slightly happier.

"I'm cutting this stone to make sure that it is square and its dimensions are uniform, so that it fits exactly in its place in a wall."

Closer to determining what the stonecutters were working on but still unclear, the traveler walked to the third stonecutter and asked him what he was doing. He was humming and was the happiest of them all.

"I'm building a cathedral," he said.

Hunt Well

Hunt what you need, and eat what you kill.

In 1974, Muhammad Ali was fighting George Foreman for the heavyweight boxing title in Kinshasa, near where you Boo and Kidogo lived. One day, a group of kids came to Ali's gym to watch him train. Ali noticed that one of them had a skull cap on his head. Ali looked at him and said, "Heh boy, why're you wearing a skull cap?"

"Because I got cancer," the boy said, "and lost my hair."

Ali knelt to the boy's height, made a fist and said, "Listen kid, I'm gonna beat Foreman, and you're gonna beat cancer."

A few weeks later, Ali heard that the boy wasn't doing so well, so Ali went to visit him in the hospital. The boy was lying in bed with tubes in him. Ali flashed his famous fist and said, "What'd I tell ya kid? I'm gonna beat Foreman, and you're gonna beat cancer."

"No," the boy said. "I'm going to heaven. I'm going to meet God, and I'm going to tell him that I know Muhammad Ali."

Is the point of winning the heavyweight title of the world, to win the heavyweight title of the world? In your life, you'll get what you take, and become what you give.

VII

HEAL

Hunting increases happiness by getting things. Healing increases happiness by dropping things.

Hunting gets bacos that get opioids that get happiness. But Want and Fear fuel the happy hunt, and the hunt costs physical, mental and emotional energy, so as you acquire bacos, you also acquire bycatch, which generates neurosis and stress. You get wounded in the fight.

Hunting bacos creates bycatch because:

1) The body releases more dopamine for wanting bacos than it releases opioids for acquiring them.[29] Meaning, you want.

2) As soon as you get something you want, your body gives you a short-term opioid hit then tells you to get more. This is known as the hedonic treadmill.[30]

3) The body probably pays more opioids for acquiring bacos than it does for keeping them. How, for example, do you feel when you first get a new bike? How do you feel about the bike a month later?

4) The more bacos you get, the less opioids your body pays you for them. The body pays you less and less

to the homeostasis point, then punishes you beyond this. Food, for example, tastes great when hungry, neutral when full, and noxious when over-consumed.[31]

Given this, the game is rigged. Working for the Narco makes us desirous but not satiated. We're chemical addicts, to ourselves. We're almost always hungry and rarely ever full. As soon as we're full, expectations rise and we're hungry again. We're never fully satisfied or tranquillo in our biological base state, without conscious management. The Narco wants you this way; addicted. Nature is greedy, because survival is mortal.

You can increase happiness by managing things outside and inside of yourself. Usually, we try to change circumstances outside ourselves to be happy inside ourselves. We try to appease the Narco and calm the Monkey by getting bacos to buy peace. When we do this, however, we almost always want and are always searching, chasing. We work for the Narco and the Monkey, and our internal happiness depends on external circumstances.

"Negative feelings are in you, not in reality. So stop trying to change reality. That's crazy! Stop trying to change the other person. We spend all our time and energy trying to change external circumstances, trying to change our spouses, our bosses, our friends, our enemies and everyone else. We don't have to change anything. Negative feelings are in you. No person on earth has the power to make you unhappy. ... Nobody told you this; they told you the opposite. ... That is why you're asleep."

— Anthony de Mello

School and work advocate this acquire-and-appease

strategy. They predominantly teach you to get, get, get. Add, add, add. Add more brains, more bank, more bacos. The more you add and manipulate external circumstances, the more "successful" you'll be. Everyone then assumes that the more successful you are, the happier you are.

Nearly every poster, sign and commercial you see reinforces this. Of all the things you see each day, how many are ads? Twenty-five percent? Walk down the street as you listen to the radio. Nearly every message you see and hear is telling you to get something and showing you how much stronger, thinner, prettier and happier you'll be if you do. Filter input.

These ads are created by the monkeys in other people's heads to try to manipulate and control the monkey in your head, so that their monkey can get bacos from you to feed their Narco to get temporary peace and happiness. The entire system is infected.

Instead of getting things, one of the quickest ways to significantly increase happiness is to drop things.

How much energy have you spent in your life trying to get things? Make a list of everything you did today. How much time was spent trying to get things? How much to drop things?

"Let go or be dragged."

— Zen saying

Hunting is fun but hard, and over time you can entangle yourself in a prison of Thoughts, Want, Fear, Identity, anger, anxiety, control, attachments and objects. Here are some tactics to drop this bycatch and get closer to escaping.[32]

Drop Thoughts

Get a pebble and a piece of ice. Think of something you're looking forward to, like a vacation, and a problem you have, like a bully. The pebble is the Thought of your vacation and the ice is the Thought of the bully. Hold the pebble in one fist and the ice in the other.

The pebble, your vacation, is happy and warm. It feels good. The ice, your bully, is sad and cold. It doesn't feel good. Now, unclench a fist and drop one of these objects. Whichever you keep, think about it for the next minute. Which do you drop, and which do you keep?

When consciously aware, you'll drop the ice and keep the pebble. You'll think about your vacation. Ironically, however, in day-to-day reality, most people drop the pebble, hold the ice and choose the bully. They sit around and stress about the bully. Why? Because they're not aware and don't choose. Their Monkey does, and the Monkey loves problems, even ones it can't fix.

"What is the most resilient parasite? Bacteria? A virus? An intestinal worm? An idea. Resilient … highly contagious. Once an idea has taken hold of the brain, it's almost impossible to eradicate."[33]

— *Inception*, Christopher Nolan

We forget that we can drop thoughts and have a hard time doing so, even when we know it's counterproductive to keep clutching them. We fight to get things. We fight to keep things. And we fight to let things go.

"Drop thoughts that don't make you strong."

— Unattributed

"You'd never invite a thief into your house. So why would you allow thoughts that steal your joy to make themselves at home in your mind?"

— Unattributed

If experiences were painful going in, they may be painful coming out. But you can drop it like a kidney stone. Release and purge it. They are just thoughts. Ideas in your head. Energy in your body. Wisps in the wind.

"Your past is just a story. Once you realize this, it has no power over you."[34]

— Chuck Palahniuk

"Don't trip over something behind you."

— Unattributed

Drop Thinking

Beyond thoughts, create gaps in the process that creates them: thinking.

The monkey mind thinks. Almost always. But how much thinking is redundant, obsessive, negative and unnecessary?

Try this: Sit down, close your eyes and let your mind think for three minutes. Let it wander like normal. After three minutes, jot down the thoughts you had. How many were productive, negative, redundant? What percentage of your thoughts are irrelevant?

When you're obsessing over something, ask yourself if

thinking about it anymore will improve it anymore. If not, change what you're looking at to change what you're thinking about. Move your head. Look at something constructive.

You can shift your mental focus by physically doing something else, particularly something that forces you into the RWAIN, like shooting, snowboarding or meditation.

Drop Want

One day, Jungle Boy was eating a coconut when Rasta Monkey said, "Coco okay, but you wanna eat inanas? I know an islan in da riva wid da tasty inanas."

"What about Crocodile?" Boy asked.

"Khul," Monkey said. "I showa someone else."

"All right, all right," Boy replied.

Monkey grabbed his bag and jumped on Boy's back. Boy got in the river and swam downstream. Halfway, they saw Crocodile's bumpy back slithering toward them.

"Swim bredda," Monkey said.

Boy swam as hard as he could. He made it to the island just as Crocodile snapped at his heels and beached his belly into the bank.

They ate bananas and fell asleep in the sun, happy and full. When they woke, Monkey said, "I know anotha islan, wid da bigger and bester inanas."

"Maybe we should go back," Boy said.

"Upstream? We barely made it here, and now you bong belly fat. If you go back, Crocodile fat."

Jungle Boy scratched his chin, then nodded. Monkey grabbed his bag and jumped on his back. He got in the river and swam downstream. Halfway, Crocodile surfaced again and slithered toward them.

"Swim bredda," Monkey said.

Boy swam hard but grew tired as Crocodile closed.

"You ate many inanas," Monkey noted.

"What's in your bag?" Boy asked, sucking air.

Just as Boy reached the island, Crocodile burst through the surface and snapped off Boy's pinky toe. Boy dragged himself ashore, trailing blood.

On shore, Boy looked at his missing toe, then grabbed Monkey's bag and ripped it open. It was full of bananas.

"Why'd we go swimming so far downstream for bananas if you already had a bag full of them?" Boy asked.

Monkey flashed monkey gum.

"I don't know," he shrugged. "But I know anotha islan."

We swim from one want island to the next, until we realize that we already have almost everything we need.

"Want what you have."

Why can a pauper be happier than a prince?

About 2,500 years ago, Siddhartha Gautama was a rich prince who lived in a palace in Northern India, near the Himalayan foothills.[35] When Siddhartha was born, his mom died giving birth to him, and a psychic told his father, the King, that Siddhartha would either become a great king or a great holy man.

Siddhartha's father wanted Siddhartha to take his place and become a king. So his father did everything he could to prevent Siddhartha from becoming a holy man. He kept Siddhartha in the palace, prevented him from leaving, gave him everything he ever wanted and kept him from seeing anyone suffer.[36]

When Siddhartha turned 29, he managed to leave the palace four times with his charioteer, Channa, despite his father's efforts. When he did, he saw an old man, a diseased man, a corpse and an ascetic. He asked Channa what was wrong with the old man, since he'd never seen one before. Channa told him that people aged and died. Siddhartha never knew this, and it disturbed him.

After these trips, Siddhartha left the palace and decided not to be the king. He became an ascetic and started a spiritual quest to become enlightened. Six years later, at 35, after trial and error, Siddhartha meditated under the Bodhi tree for 49 days. He battled the demon Mara, lord of ego and illusion, and became "the enlightened one," or Buddha.

After obtaining nirvana, Buddha spent seven weeks alone, then gave a lecture to five ascetics on what became known as the Four Noble Truths, the core of Buddhism. These are:

1) Life is suffering.

2) The cause of suffering is desire (Want).

3) Suffering can be cured by eliminating desire.

4) To remove desire, follow the eight-fold path:

> Right Understanding
> Right Intent
> Right Speech
> Right Action
> Right Livelihood
> Right Effort
> Right Mindfulness
> Right Concentration

Thus, one of Buddhism's main objectives is to minimize Want, to decrease suffering and increase happiness.

Can you completely eliminate Want? As long as you're in leopard skin you need food and water. And if you eliminate want for everything but food and water, you won't suffer much, but you probably won't smile much either. How fun would it be to just want food and water? Also, if you eliminate Want to get spiritual enlightenment, you simply trade wants, swapping a desire for physical bacos for a desire for mental bacos. Monks still want something: non-want. Evolution has engineered you to want. Want is inescapable.

But do some things you want make you unhappy? You can probably make yourself 3 percent happier immediately just by eliminating or minimizing some obsessive, compulsive, habitual want fat. Do the vents have to be spotless? Do drinks need coasters? Hedgerows defended? Drivers beat? Games won? Arguments won? Positions defended? Bikes orange? Wrongs avenged? Rivals hurt?

Politicians heard? Outcomes controlled? Cigarettes smoked? Speeches perfect? Everything perfect?

Make a list of things that annoy you. Would you be happier if you just ignored some of these things? On a larger scale, cross-check your want list. Do you have to have each thing on it? Would you be happier if you simply didn't want some of them?

"To become rich: get more or want less."

— Unattributed

A pauper can be happier than a prince, because happiness comes from both getting something and experiencing it. A sailboat alone won't make you happy. You have to consume and appreciate it. Your experience of it differs if you're a castaway or a king. You control half of the happiness equation. Actually, you control most of it, because you also influence what you get.

Drop Fear

Fear drives and limits you. People drive spikes in the dark to keep fear out, until they've driven so many that they've locked themselves in. They cower around dying fires, entombed with the idea of fear, which is greater than the fear itself, never wondering, "How can I be smaller than something I created?"

"Care about what other people think, and you will always be their prisoner."

— Lao Tzu

You create your own fear. Once you realize this, you

can control and dissipate it better. Fear, however, is irrational, and even if you know that a fear is senseless and counterproductive, you can still feel and experience it strongly. This is natural and okay. Because fear is biologically engineered into you like a muscle. Humanoids who petted lions were eaten long ago.

Turn on fear. Force yourself to do things you fear.

"Everything you want, lies on the other side of fear."

— Unattributed

Attacking fear defeats it. Running from it empowers it. Like the monkeys at Matheran: Show strength, monkey brake. Show fear, monkey take.

"I have spent my whole life scared. Frightened of things that could happen, might happen, might not happen. Fifty years I spent like that. Finding myself awake at three in the morning. But you know what, ever since my diagnosis I sleep just fine. I came to realize it's that fear that's the worst of it. That's the real enemy. So get up, get out in the real world and kick that bastard as hard as you can right in the teeth."

— *Breaking Bad*, Vince Gilligan, Moira Walley-Beckett, Thomas Schnauz, George Mastras, Peter Gould and Sam Catlin

Drop Identity

Is it tiring to always be Super Mom, Macho, Proper, the Boss, the Leader, the Jock, the Jester, the Genius, the Model, the Life of the Party?

To camouflage our weaknesses and hide who we hate, we project who we aren't, entirely. We're always projecting. You're projecting at people and they're projecting at you. Tricking, faking and hiding like debutants at the derby, or chameleons in the jungle. Pretending to be people we're not. Perfect people. It's tiring.

Our Identity is heavy. Frequently, we don't even realize we're carrying it. When we do, we're too intimidated by Fear to drop it.

"Tension is who you think you should be. Relaxation is who you are."

— Chinese Proverb

What's the distance between your résumé self and your home alone in the middle of the night with whiskey online self? This distance is your projection. The greater the distance and the longer you hold it, the heavier your armor. We drink and act out to escape the weight of our pretend selves.

We have to project. You can't go to court nude and win, and you shouldn't expose your weaknesses to a predator, like a terrorist. But we can lighten our armor and let down our guard at times.

The less you have to project, the happier you'll be. People probably project 75 percent more than necessary. What do you love in your best friends? Frequently, it's their vulnerabilities, faults and scars, because these make them human, like us. Good people love these things in you, too.

Be yourself as much as you can. If you want to paint your nails, do it for the people who will like it instead of fearing those who will judge you. You are who you are, and people can take it or leave it.

Find a spouse who likes you for who you really are, who knows and likes your strengths and weaknesses. Know their secrets, and let them know yours.

If so, you'll have your own shared secret, which will warm you like a fire in winter, and you'll conspire like collaborators with a map to buried treasure. If not, you'll lay bricks on a bad sightline, and the Berlin Wall will eventually transect you, with old roads that end at odd angles.

Sometimes you have to project at work, but don't at home. It's too tiring. If so, you'll always be alone, drinking with yourself in an empty bar on Christmas Eve.

Be up-front with your spouse. The sooner the better. What's easier, telling someone you just met a secret about yourself or telling them 10 years into a marriage, after you've formed an identity that they've built a house upon?

Try the secret game. Within the first 30 seconds of meeting an attractive stranger, when you're both still the perfect projection of each other's dream, and the reality of them is still better than the idea of them, tell them a secret about yourself and ask them for one about them. The stark honesty is so frightening and refreshing that you realize how guarded you always are. If they embrace this, that is, if they embrace you, great. If they turn and run, great; you just saved yourself 10 years.

Lastly, let your spouse be themselves. Love them for who they are and their faults instead of trying to judge, critique and change them into your projection of them. Be a harbor in the storm. This is hard. A lot of this is hard.

Drop Anger

Life isn't fair. You'll be robbed and cheated. You'll get angry. It's okay. It's impossible not to. Sometimes, you've got to.

"There is a huge amount of freedom that comes to you when you take nothing personally."[37]

— Don Miguel Ruiz

What's important is how you handle anger. Don't react; respond. The person who frequently wins social confrontations is the one who responds with the least emotion and most tactical patience.

When you're angry, ask yourself: "Will anger help me here? Is this worth being angry over? If so, what's the best way to channel it?"

Drop anger as soon as it is no longer productive to be angry. As soon as you no longer obtain productive motivation from anger, you get unhappiness from it. The thief stole your wallet, then he steals your peace. The wallet is gone. Vaya con Dios. Look for the opportunity in the situation, rather than the injustice.

"Holding onto anger is like holding onto a hot coal with the intent of throwing it at someone else. You're the one who gets burnt."[38]

— Possibly paraphrased from Emmet Fox

Drop Anxiety

What percentage of the things you worry about actually

happen? Maybe they don't happen because you worry about them. Regardless, how much worry does it take to prevent or resolve a problem, and how much extra, unnecessary worry do you oversalt beyond this?

What if you could get back all the time you wasted worrying or being unhappy? How much time would it be? What would you do with it? I'd probably get a decade of my life back.

Next time you're worrying, ask yourself, "In 10 years, will I wish I had this time back as free, bonus time to use any way I wanted?" If so, why not take that time now?

The mind exists to solve problems, "so it wants everything to be a problem."[39]

— David Cain

Like fear, anger and general thinking, worry about something until it is no longer helpful to do so, then drop it like dry ice. Decide on the course of action for the problem, then stop thinking about it. Take any problem you have right now and ask yourself, "Is it helping to keep thinking about this?" If not, drop it.

How? Try this.

The Monkey always has to have a problem. It has to work on something. Can you remember a time in your life when your Monkey wasn't worrying about something?

Problems are constructive or destructive. Constructive problems are enjoyable and positive. Working on a puzzle is constructive. Destructive problems are unenjoyable and negative. Worrying about how to get revenge on a bully who wronged you is destructive. It's a negative event that creates more negativity the more you think about it.

Think about problems like tangible things inside you. The problem is an acorn in your head, and its anxiety is rooted in your limbs. Take an empty bottle and write the name of the destructive problem that's bothering you on it. For example, "Will my class like my speech?" or just "Speech." Open the lid, set it in front of you and sit. Close your eyes and fix yourself in the present by listening to the birds, rain, leaves or wind.

Once present, accept the problem. It exists. I can't solve it anymore for now. It isn't making me happy and I want to be done with it. Then, when you breathe in, grab the acorn in your mind and the roots in your limbs. When you breathe out, pull the acorn and roots out of you. Put them in front of you, in the bottle. The problem came from inside you, from your mind, so put it outside you. Take big breaths, grabbing the acorn and roots and putting them in the bottle. As you breathe, ask yourself if it will do any good to keep thinking about the problem. Do I want to be done with it? Do I want to be happy?

Once the problem is in the bottle, cap it. Make the cap a positive thought, so later when you see something that reminds you of the problem (my class judging me), think of the cap (Mom congratulating me with a hug) instead.

Take the bottle and set it on a shelf. "Look Monkey, here's the problem. It still exists. This is where it is, and you can worry about it later if needed. I'm not denying it. I'm just setting it aside for now." The Monkey hates to let problems go.

Now take a pebble and put it in your pocket. The pebble is a constructive problem. For example, "How would I design a video game?"

Every time the destructive problem boomerangs back into your mind, think of the bottle, the cap and the pebble, and talk to the Monkey: "Monkey, the problem is bottled and capped on the shelf. It's actually going to be a good thing, with Mom hugging me, but we're not thinking about it until we figure out how to design our video game." Play with the pebble in your hand, and move the Monkey from the destructive problem to the constructive one.

Redirecting your awareness helps, but you will likely still retain the problem until you accept the new reality, loss or hit. Then you can drop it and advance. Sometimes you have to admit you've lost to win. Know when to fight and when to flow.

One evening, two monks were returning to a monastery. It had rained and the road was wet. At one spot, a beautiful women stood in front of a puddle, unable to cross it. The monks were not allowed to touch women, but the elder monk lifted her, carried her across the puddle and set her on the other side. The young monk watched in disbelief. A minute later, they continued on.

Later that night at the monastery, the young monk said, "Sir, we cannot touch women, right?"

"Yes," the elder monk said.

"But then, sir, why did you pick the young women up?"

The elder monk smiled. "I left her on the other side of the puddle, but you are still carrying her."

Drop Control

Focus on things you can control, disregard the rest.

"The more concerned we become over the things we can't control, the less we will do the things we can control."

— John Wooden

Even with the things you can control, you can't control everything. Everything usually won't be perfect (as defined by you), and that's okay. Release expectation and see what happens when you don't try to control every outcome. Accept, appreciate and relax. Nothing is under control.

"Chasing after the world brings chaos. Allowing it to come to me brings peace."

— Zen Gatha

Take your want list and look at it again in 10 years. See if you're happy that you didn't get some of the things on it that you wanted, like a Honda CRX with 10-inch woofers. Life is looking out for you more than you think. Everything will be okay.

Many years ago, there was a great Zen master in Japan named Hakuin. All his neighbors praised him for living a pure life.

One day, the parents of a beautiful Japanese girl discovered that she was pregnant. They were very angry. They demanded to know who the father was. At first, she refused to name him, but after much harassment she named Hakuin.

In great anger, the parents went to the Zen master and confronted him. "Is that so?" was all Hakuin said.

When the baby was born, the parents gave the baby to

Hakuin. By then, he had lost his reputation, which did not trouble him.

Hakuin took good care of the baby. He obtained milk and raised the baby well.

A year later, the girl confessed that Hakuin was not the father. The real father was a young man who worked in the fish market.

The parents immediately went to Hakuin and apologized. They begged for forgiveness and asked for the baby back. Hakuin gave the baby back and said, "Is that so?"

Drop Boats

Enjoy the physical commodities you earn, like your video games and computer, but remember that sometimes less is more. If you want a boat, calculate what you'll have to pay in time, energy and worry to keep it. As soon as someone wins the lottery, they have to protect it.

Who is richer, the monk or the millionaire?

"The things you own end up owning you. It's only after you lose everything that you're free to do anything."[40]

— Chuck Palahniuk

Drop Attachment

If our house was on fire and you could only save five things other than your family, what would you save? Make a list.

As noted, when you were first born, you were frequently attached to Mom. As you move outward from her to your room, the house, the park, kindergarten, friends and beyond, you attach to different things, like jumping across rocks in a river. You shift from Mom to friends, games, music, identities, ideas, wants, fears, spouses and kids. You're always attached to something. Even guys who move to a cabin in Alaska to write manifestos about detaching from society have attached themselves to the idea of detachment. And an Identity.

We live like we're going to live forever, like all these things we have and grip are permanent. Our house, our friends, our spouse. They're ours and only ours. How can they not be? We fought so hard for them, and spent so much blood and treasure to get them. We own them and will forever. But will we? Can we ever really possess anything?

Someday, all these things will leave your life. Your career, your house, your land, your friends, your spouse. Look around you. Look at everything you have. You will have none of these things. They'll go, like sand castles and thieves, like a dog let out, who one day doesn't come home. Where was that sock? What was her name? They'll disintegrate in your grip, then in your memory. Everything will be taken from you, as it was given to you, until the only thing that remains is your rib naked life, gasping like a fish in the shadow of Death.

"Ashes to ashes. Dust to dust."

Buddhists believe that attachment causes suffering, because we attach to things we think are permanent but aren't.

"Most of our troubles are due to our passionate desire

for and attachment to things that we misapprehend as enduring entities."[41]

— The Dalai Lama

Buddha taught that liberation from suffering comes when we detach ourselves from transient things — that we only lose what we cling to.

Take this for what it's worth. Attach and detach to what you like, to the degree you like. Attachment awareness alone can decrease suffering and increase happiness, because people frequently attach to malignant ideas and problems. We frequently attach to whatever passes by, bouncing from one attachment to the next, unconsciously driven by Want and Fear, wondering why things never go our way.

Attach to people and love. Detach from anger and hate. I'm forever attached to you, and this is worth anything.

What were the five things you saved from the fire? These are things you've already attached to. You've probably put energy and life-time into them. They're tangible manifestations of the bacos you value most, and they're probably healthy attachments that generate happiness.

Did you save anything negative from the fire? Anything that causes anxiety, anger or resentment? Like something unfair that happened to you? Probably not. So why stay attached to negative energy in daily interactions, like we do? If you wouldn't save your anger over that injustice from the fire, why keep tangling with it every day?

You can probably quickly increase happiness by

detaching from some petty negative drama, habits and thoughts. If you get angry every morning listening to political talk radio on the way to work, and you can't channel that anger into anything constructive, why do it?

Someday, for example, someone will break up with you and break your heart. Let them go as quickly as you can. Are you going to have accepted the reality of the new situation and forgotten them in 10 years? Then why not accept the reality now and forget them in 10 minutes? If the outcome is the same, why add suffering to it?

Yet we do, because we frequently refuse to accept a new reality and detach from circumstances that no longer exist. The money is stolen, the game is lost, the girlfriend ran off, the friend is dead. Yes, you were robbed, beaten, betrayed and hurt. But until you let these injustices go, they will continue to rob, beat, betray and hurt you. When you lock-jaw on them like a crazed dog who fights to the death, sometimes you do. Then you're not connected to a set of fixable variables. You're attached to a Thought. An Idea. A ghost space that only you haunt.

"As I walked out the door to the gate that would lead me to freedom, I knew if I didn't leave my bitterness and hatred behind, I'd still be in prison."

— Nelson Mandela

To help surmount negative external changes like these, ask yourself, "Have the circumstances changed, and can I do anything anymore to change them?" If not, accept and advance. Otherwise, you might as well worry about how to keep the moon from falling from the sky. Almost all time spent being unhappy, after ventilating energy or defending territory, is wasted.

A few years ago, one of my marine biology professors was working on an oil rig off the Gulf Coast. Sometimes, he and some other workers would freedive off the rig and spearfish to catch their dinner. They spearfished around the pillars, because these provided the only points of reference in the deep blue ocean, and fish formed vertical communities around them. Each time they dove, they naturally used to see who could spear the biggest fish.

One day, the workers saw a huge grouper rise from the depths. Excited, a worker plunged for it and shot it through the eye, killing it instantly. He smiled up at his buddies. But then the fish began to sink. His spear, which was stuck through the grouper's eye, was tethered on a rope to his wrist so that he didn't lose it when he shot and missed in the open water.

Instead of cutting the line, the worker tried to swim against the sinking fish and surface it. Initially, he made progress, and moved for the surface. But the fish was big, and its time was done. Running out of breath and being pulled down, the worker stopped kicking up and frantically searched for his knife latched to his ankle. He inverted and began to follow the fish down as he clutched for his knife. His friends watched him disappear into the dark blue.

They never saw him again.

Dad School

VIII

MANAGE

Above discussed ways to get bacos and drop bycatch — how to hunt and heal.

Below are three ways to manage steps in the happiness drug deal. You can manage the thoughts, perception and players in the process to increase happiness.

Thought Control

As stated, the Narco can't entirely tell the difference between a physical object, like a hyena, and a Thought, like a dream of a hyena. Both objects and thoughts can be real to him. A Thought can produce a physical chemical reaction, and the Narco will release opioids for it.

Take a second, for example, and picture that upcoming vacation. What will you do? Where will you eat? What will you drink? What will you see?

Now, how do you feel? You got a happiness hit, and nothing external changed. You didn't move, and nothing entered your body. You haven't physically experienced the vacation yet, but you enjoy the thought of it, because you mentally experience it, which is how the physical experience is ultimately imprinted anyway.

Likewise, thoughts hurt. Is someone more likely to be killed by a lion or themselves? Lions attack about 600 people every year. About 40,000 Americans killed themselves last year. About five people blow themselves to good riddance every day in Iraq for jihad. For an idea. For a Thought. Ideas kill more people than fangs. You're more dangerous to yourself than a lion.

"An idea is like a virus. Resilient, highly contagious. The smallest seed of an idea can grow. It can grow to define or destroy you."[42]

— *Inception*, Christopher Nolan

The fact that a Thought alone can produce happiness (or sadness) is a significant exploitable loophole in the happiness process. It is because, unlike external factors, you can create and control your thoughts. A Thought cannot get in your head without you letting it in, or without you creating it and letting it stay. Thoughts are guests. They're not you, landlords or squatters.

Thoughts influence and change us. If you're going to shoot the game winning free throw, for example, your coach can tell you, "Don't be a donkey!" and don't miss it, or "Be a hero!" and make it. Both outcomes are possible: missing the shot or making it. But right as you're standing at the line about to shoot, is it better to have the hero thought or the fail thought flash through your head?

Despite the impact that thoughts have on our moods, successes and lives, we usually aren't independently aware of them and don't try to manage them. Instead, we frequently react to triggers, attach to whatever thought pops in our heads, and zombie-follow it down thought chains into thought pits.

Imagine, for example, that you're on a tropical beach. Serrated palm shadows flicker in sand. The sand squeezes between your toes. The sun warms your skin. The air smells like salt. Then you see a dirty diaper wash ashore. Your Monkey analyzes, loads, thinks and judges. "That's gross. People should be more respectful. If the locals just cleaned up. That local waiter overcharged me at lunch. ..."

Everything is perfecto, and you worked all year to engineer these perfecto circumstances to put yourself on this perfecto playa, yet in two seconds you're unhappy. You're miles from the beach mentally. You're an upset victim thinking about a possible past injustice that you can't do anything about and has no physical connection to the present.

Likewise, what happens when a song comes on the radio that reminds you of your ex-girlfriend, or you see a fast food sign? Songs and symbols trigger thought chains and emotions, which is why companies create them. They try to exploit this mental vulnerability to trigger a thought chain that ends with you giving them something.

The Monkey is easily mislead. What is the biggest problem you have now? Does it have to do with a person? How does it make you feel?

See, three questions on one subject and your awareness shifts to a negative thought that just stole some of your happiness like a cat-burglar. It stole a few seconds of your life. You could have done anything with that time; instead, you spent it agitated.

If we're hungry, do we eat? If we're sick, do we take medicine? If we're tired, do we sleep? If we're on safari, do we keep our distance from lions? Yes. Yet if we're depressed, what do we do? Frequently, nothing. Instead of running from the lion we hug it. We sulk and wait for external factors to change. We wait for the lion to vanish. Or, more proactively, we try to solve the problem by changing external factors. This is like holding a taco and saying, "I won't eat this taco and feel better until Barbar apologizes! And I get a good parking spot." What does Barbar have to do with your taco? Eat it.

Not managing your thoughts is like standing in the sleet when you can walk inside. If someone is in a bad mood, it's either chemically driven, which happens and plays a significant role in happiness, but isn't discussed here, or they're possessed by a negative thought they can't exorcise.

A great power you have is the ability to choose one thought over another.[43] You can frequently, simply, choose to be happier. Do you want to keep being unhappy? Then keep thinking about what's making you unhappy. Do you want to be happy? Think about what makes you happy.

To manage thoughts, first be aware of them. Simple, but many people aren't. Then, notice triggers and break negative thought chains. Drop destructive thoughts and replace them with happy ones. Think about the sand in your toes instead of the diaper.

Feed the Narco the bacos in happy thoughts instead of the bacos in tangible objects. Trick him. Happy thoughts are free. You don't have to go out and get them or change the world. You can self-generate an inexhaustible supply of them.

Because Mother Nature is a slave driver, negative thoughts have more gravity and higher escape velocities than positive thoughts, so it helps to keep several positive thoughts in-pocket every day. What's a happy thought you have right now? Write it down and put it in your pocket. When the Monkey starts to wander and worry down a negative thought chain, stop him, or let him run his course to purge the energy, then think about your happy thought and redirect the Monkey to a constructive problem. Every morning in the shower, plot and pocket a happy thought. Swim back to it several times a day to stay afloat.

The exit to Happiness is so evident that we frequently miss it. You already have almost everything you need for everything you want. You just don't realize it.

Perception

Complete this sentence; The glass is half _____.

If you're in an optimistic mood, the glass looks half full. If you're in a pessimistic mood, it looks half empty. But here's the important point: It's both. Your perception of it determines what it becomes, like Schrödinger's cat.

Appreciate what you get. Why get it if you don't? A raft is a raft but to a castaway and a king.

Likewise, center your frame of reference. Too tired to work out? You're lucky you have legs.

People create many of their own problems. Once, Grandpa told me to sweep the patio when I was a kid. I didn't want to do it and got mad. I picked up a cheap metal patio chair, spun and threw it. It bounced off the brick wall and flew back into my face. It broke my front tooth in half. This created a series of negative events that I was still paying for 30 years later at the dentist's office in India.

A tree falls on your bike and breaks it. Who created the problem? The tree, I guess. But your reaction to this event, and everything after it, is on you. This is a decision you make at a decision point.

You make yourself happy or unhappy. Success begets success. Failure begets failure. There is good and bad in every situation. You can focus on the good and be happy, or focus on the bad and be unhappy. In India, half the diplomats are happy and want to extend their tours. Half are unhappy and want to come home. India remains the same throughout. But you can try to change it if you want.

Once, a woman watched a dog walk into a room. A minute later, the dog came out smiling and wagging his tail. Another dog then walked into the room, and a minute later he came out growling.

Wondering what could make one dog so happy and the other so mad, the woman walked into the room. To her surprise, she found a room filled with mirrors.

The happy dog found a thousand happy dogs looking back at him, while the angry dog found a thousand angry dogs growling at him.

Who you are reflects what you see in the world, and what you give the world determines what returns to you.

Like a mouthful of metal chair.

There is a similar story in Aesop's Fables.[44] It's such an old story that a philosopher refers to it in circa 500 BC, 2,500 years ago.[45] It's called "The Dog and His Reflection,":

One day, a dog stole a bone. He fled and came to a river. Before crossing the river, he looked down at the water. He saw his own reflection in it but thought that this was another dog carrying something better, so he barked at it. When he did, he opened his mouth, dropped his bone in the river and lost it.

An illustration of "The Dog and its Reflection"
from an edition of Aesop's fables; 1564.

Players

Manage the players in the happiness process.

The Leopard: As noted, your body requires some base physical needs. If you're unhealthy, hungry, thirsty, cold or chemically unbalanced, you can't focus on deeper fulfillment. Keep healthy and chemically balanced.

Exercise. Exercise creates neurons and releases endorphins that produce happiness.[46] Studies indicate that exercise makes people happier over time.

Sleep. Sleep helps your body repair, recover and produce. Studies indicate that sleep deprivation negatively impacts the part of your brain that recalls positive memories (hippocampus) more than it negatively impacts the part that recalls negative memories (amygdala). This means that when you lack sleep, it's harder to produce positive thoughts than negative thoughts. You're grumpy.[47]

The Storm: It's okay to be angry and unhappy. I am. Everyone is. Let your emotions flow through you. Don't contain them; direct them. Use them constructively. Do push-ups instead of punching your brother. Thoughts and emotions are symbiotic. Sometimes a thought creates an emotion, and sometimes an emotion creates a thought. When you pick up a thought, you pick up the emotional vine wrapped around it.

The Monkey: As noted, the Monkey exists to solve problems, so give him constructive problems to work on, like how to design a video game. If you don't, he'll find his own problems and kidnap you for the emotional ride. Either you work for your Monkey, or he works for you.

Reestablish Awareness and re-center yourself. Take five minutes every day to sever consciousness and not work on a problem with the Monkey. It's surprisingly hard to do. Think about that. Nearly every waking minute, every day, for our entire lives, we're trying to solve a problem. And many are unsolvable, pointless problems that depress us. How much time and consciousness have you wasted trying to mentally change unchangeable hard points? Set the alarm on your phone to repeat at a certain time every day. When it goes off, see if you're thinking about a problem. Is it constructive and worth your time and happiness?

Or try another consciousness exercise: Every morning as soon as you start to cross the border between half-sleep and waking up, like as you fully wake in the shower, try to consciously stop for a few seconds. Stall at the sleep frontier and observe. As hazy dreams burn off, you'll see yourself subconsciously reattaching to yesterday's problem set, which is laying there like heavy armor for you to put back on from the night before. Also notice that whatever first thought or emotion you haphazardly leap into at that moment frequently sets your mood for the next few hours.

Try to manage this morning mind meld. Rise into waking consciousness, but enjoy the presence for a minute before starting the next 16-hour problem cycle. Feel hot water hit your neck. Hear it drip off you. Feel your toes on the tile. Then consciously attach to a constructive problem in a positive mood to point your ship in the right direction.

Identity: If you create a victim identity, you'll have to feed it with misfortune.

"So many humans are suffering because of false images we try to project. Humans pretend to be something very important, but at the same time we believe we are nothing. We work so hard to be someone in that society Dream, to be recognized and approved by others. We try so hard to be important, to be a winner, to be powerful, to be rich, to be famous … and to impose our dream … Why? Because humans believe the dream is real, and we take it very seriously."

— Don Miguel Ruiz

91

Love yourself.

"Imagine that you love yourself just the way you are. You love your body just the way it is, and you love your emotions just the way they are. You know that you are perfect just the way you are."

— Don Miguel Ruiz

Hero and Shadow: Constrain both. There's a story that when Caesar used to walk into the Forum to speak to the people, a servant would whisper in his ear:

"Always remember that you're merely a man."

Forgive yourself.

In Sum

You'll spend years trying to control, manipulate and "improve" external circumstances to make yourself happy. "Once I get a raise, I'll be happy. … Once I get a new car, I'll be set ..." We do this, and should constantly strive to improve ourselves and the world.

Simultaneously, however, remember that change and happiness aren't as correlated as imagined, because not only do you have to struggle to make the change occur, but as soon as you do, the mind has to experience it. As soon as this happens and you've gotten what you want, you reset the goal posts farther out. What's easier, changing the external world or changing your internal experience of it?

As the swordsman Miyamoto Musashi wrote in circa 1645:

"There is nothing outside of yourself that can ever enable you to get better, stronger, richer, quicker or smarter. Everything is within. Everything exists. Seek nothing outside of yourself."[48]

Dad School

IX

FLOW

The day destroys the night
The night divides the day
Tried to run
Tried to hide
Break on through to the other side

— The Doors

Have you ever watched fish in a stream and wondered if they realize what a vast world exists beyond their surface? Beyond their eddies and fish telenovelas? What can they deduce from watery light, raindrops and dead bugs? How far can Fish Einstein get? Can he imagine cobra charmers in Marrakech, or gogo girls in Bangkok? Can he sense the rubbery ridges on the top of a mastiff's mouth, or the giant rain drops in Copán? The fish probably don't bother, and the stream remains their world entire.

Hunt, heal and manage the happiness process to increase happiness, as detailed. You'll be happy. You'll smile. You'll score fish touchdowns with your fish friends. But realize that your happy hunt occurs in a stream, and water flows through it like time. Shatter the boundaries, and realize that you can operate outside this process and transcend the stream for deeper meaning and purpose.

Even the alleged boundaries, where are they? Where are you in being, space, time and consciousness?

Being

You were created from microscopic DNA, from stardust, from almost nothing. From as close to nothing as you can get until it somehow flips and becomes something.

There's a Buddhist story that says that the chances of you existing are about the same as you throwing a ring somewhere in all the oceans on earth, and those oceans only have one turtle living in them, and this one turtle only surfaces once every 100 years, and he surfaces right in the middle of where you threw your ring, at the exact time you threw it.[49]

Surprisingly, this story is statistically plausible. Dr. Ali Binazir, for example, made the following assumptions to estimate the chance of someone (you) existing: The chance of Mom and I meeting was 1 in 20,000. The chances of Mom getting pregnant was 1 in 2,000. Sperm and eggs are genetically unique. So scientifically, only one sperm in my body had half of you in it, and only one egg in Mom's body had half of you in it. The chances of that sperm and that egg meeting and combining were 1 in 400 quadrillion.

For this already unlikely event to happen, however, it also had to happen to me, Mom, Grandpa Mike, Gramy Grandpa Steve, Grandma Gail, Great Grandpa Don, and every single one of your ancestors, all the way back to when we were single-celled organisms floating in primordial soup 4 billion years ago. If you only calculate back 150,000 generations, to the first humanoids, the possibility of every single one of your humanoid ancestors surviving recurring plagues, pestilence, famines and sieges, living to reproductive age, meeting someone and reproducing before death is 1 in $10^{2,685,000}$.

By comparison, the number of atoms in the average male is about 10^{27}, the number of atoms in earth is about 10^{50}, and the number of atoms in the universe is about 10^{80}.

Put another way, Dr. Binazir notes that given these assumptions and calculations, the chances of you existing are about equal to having everyone in San Diego (2 million people) each roll a trillion-sided dice, and each rolling the exact same number, like 550,343,279,001.[50]

Thus, you are incredibly improbable. So improbable that you can disregard probability entirely. You shouldn't exist. But do.

Where are you in space?

Space: Within

As noted, when you're a grown adult, you'll consist of about 10^{27} atoms. A lot. But atoms are small. About one-tenth of a millionth of a millimeter across. That is, if you string a million atoms together in a row, they will only span the width of a single hair on your head. There are about 7.5 trillion carbon atoms in the period at the end of this sentence.[51]

Despite this, atoms are predominantly empty. They're composed of a nucleus and a sphere-like electron cloud, which is created by orbiting electrons at probable positions. The distance between the nucleus and its farthest orbiting electrons is large. If an atom in your body was magnified to the size of a football stadium, the nucleus would be the size of a pea on the 50-yard line, and the electrons (at their outer orbital edge) would be the size of gnats, whizzing around the stadium's outer edges. Everything in between is empty space, as far as we know.

Thus, you're predominantly composed of empty space. 99.9999999999999% of you is empty space. If we could remove all of that empty space so that you were only composed of nuclei and electrons, you would be much smaller than a grain of salt. If we removed all of that empty space in every human, every human on the planet would fit into one sugar cube.

If your fist is mostly empty space, then why doesn't it go through your brother's stomach, which is also 99.9999999999999% empty space, when you gut-check him? Because forces repel them. Forces, not mass, make mass solid. We believe an oak exists because we can see and hit it, but that oak is primarily composed of forces we can't see.

"For my ally is the Force. And a powerful ally it is. Life creates it, makes it grow. Its energy surrounds us and binds us. Luminous beings are we. Not this crude matter."[52]

— *Star Wars*, George Lucus, Leigh Brackett, Lawrence Kasdan

Space: Without

From 2003 to 2014, NASA photographed a small area of space in the Fornax constellation with the Hubble

Space Telescope. NASA chose this area for its lack of close stars.

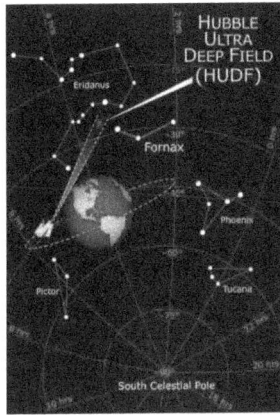

Source: NASA, ESA, S. Beckwith (STScI) and the HUDF Team.[53]

In 2014, NASA released an image of this area, compiled from several previous photographs in various wavelengths. The image is called the Hubble Ultra Deep Field 2014 (HUDF 2014).

NASA's HUDF 2014 photograph. Source: NASA, ESA, H. Teplitz and M. Rafelski (IPAC/Caltech), A. Koekemoer (STScI), R. Windhorst (ASU) and Z. Levay (STScI).[54]

As can be seen, the area in the square in the second picture appears predominantly empty to the naked eye. The HUDF 2014 image, however, reveals that it contains more than 10,000 galaxies. Each point of light in the photograph is a galaxy.[55] Each galaxy contains billions of stars. A lot, considering we orbit just one star.

Each light dot is a galaxy. Source: NASA, ESA, S. Beckwith (STScI) and the HUDF Team.[56]

Nothing has ever been photographed farther than the galaxies in this photograph. These galaxies are so far that it took the light from some of them 13 billion light-years to reach Hubble's camera. That's a long time, especially when nothing travels faster than light, which travels at 186,000 miles a second. It takes you four months to drive 186,000 miles (at 60 miles per hour). Light travels the same distance in one second. This is about 7 times around earth. Put another way, these galaxies are so far that even though light can travel around the earth 7 times in one second, it still took them 13 billion years to reach earth.

Given this, when you look at this photograph, you're looking back in time. To the origins of the universe. You're seeing light that left its destination 13 billion years ago. You're not seeing the galaxies as they are now, because they're so far away that their current light hasn't reached us yet, but as they were up to 13 billion years ago. Thus, some of the stars in the photograph may no longer exist. Only their ghost image does.

Put another way, long after you die, your image, from all visibly divisible times in your life, will radiate on, outward through space, at 186,000 miles a second. When you were born, for example, it would have taken someone standing on Pluto (an average of 3.57 billion miles from earth) five hours to see you being born — as the light of your presence traveled outward. When you turn 10, someone 58 trillion miles away, at that same moment, would not see you turning 10; they would see you being born. Likewise, someone even farther away, with a powerful enough magnifying glass, could watch you be born and the days of your life after that, long after you've already died.[57]

It is also interesting that the area in the HUDF image is incredibly small. It's just one thirteenth-millionth the size of the observable universe. If the observable universe was the size of quarter, the actual universe would be the size of earth.[58] The HUDF image captures just one thirteenth-millionth of an area of that quarter.

Given this, scientists estimate that there are between 100 billion and 200 billion galaxies in the universe.[59] A lot. Our galaxy alone, the Milky Way, has about 300 billion stars.[60] Around these stars in the Milky Way, there are about 11 billion Earth-size planets that orbit sun-like stars in the habitable zone.[61] That means there are (very) roughly 1.1e+21 planets in the universe like Earth. Again, a lot. Even if only one out of every 100,000,000,000 of these planets contains life, that means 11,000,000,000 contain life. Most probably wouldn't contain intelligent life, but it's still reasonable to speculate that it is statistically likely that we are not alone in the universe.

Time

Where are you in time?

"No man ever steps in the same river twice. For it's not the same river, and he's not the same man."

— Heraclitus

Once, in circa 1986, when I was about 12, I was sitting with Gramy and your Great-Great-Grandfather Bubba in his living room in Detroit. Bubba was about 86. After sitting with him for about 15 minutes, he looked at me and asked Gramy (his granddaughter), "Who's that?"

"That's your great-grandson, Bubba. You know him," she said.

He was old and losing his mind. He'd seen me numerous times for 12 years. He nodded and leaned back in his chair, sitting in his suit and tie, considering what Grammy had said. He wore a suit and tie every day, even though he had retired long ago and didn't leave the house much. After a minute, he pointed his finger at me and said, "In America, you can do anything you want in your life. Anything. If you put your mind to it." The way he emphasized "anything" made me remember it. This is the only thing I ever remember him saying. So this is the only thing from him and the span of his life that I can directly pass on to you. Three sentences. But they're important, and he's right.

Bubba was born in 1900 and died in 1996. He thus lived through most of the 20th century. When he was born, there were no cars, TVs or computers. He milked cows on a farm. By the time he died in 1996, there were nuclear bombs, cell phones and the internet. When he was three, the Wright brothers flew for the first time. When he was 41, the Japanese bombed Pearl Harbor. When he was 69, we put a man on the moon. Today, "your cell phone has more computer power than all of NASA had in 1969," when it put a man on the moon.[62] Neil Armstrong was a brave man.

Bubba experienced an incredible amount of change in his life, particularly compared to his ancestors. His parents didn't experience as much change, and his grandparents, in the 1800s, experienced even less. Growth is exponential.

"In the next 100 years, you'll experience 1,000 years of change."

— Michio Kaku

Homo erectus evolved 2 million years ago. For

1,988,000 years, Homo erectus, then our direct ancestors Homo sapiens (250,000 years ago), hunted and foraged like animals, walking about 12 miles a day and undergoing selection pressure for genes that could outwit a dangerous, fluid landscape. We thought, ate, killed and were culled on the move. Then, 15,000 years ago, we domesticated plants and animals. We progressed from using muscle energy to plant and animal energy, which added excess energy and bacos to our tribes, allowing us to settle into villages, work less, replicate more and spend surplus calories on art and innovation. The wheel (3,500 years ago)[63], bronze (5,300 years ago), industrial revolution (300 years ago), steam engine (200 years ago), electric motor (191 years ago), coal-fired electric generating station (130 years ago), and nuclear power plant (70 years ago) added additional energy to our societies, allowing us to do more and move less.

If this change, from 2 million years ago to 15,000 years ago (villages) to 44 years ago (the invention of the office cubicle) was proportional to 1 year, then we roamed the plains for most of the last year, settled into villages 3 days ago and only sat down in an office cubicle 12 minutes ago.

Taking it further, the universe began 13.7 billion years ago. If this and the above milestones were proportional to 1 year, than the universe began a year ago, humans began 9.59 minutes ago, we settled in villages 34 seconds ago, we sat down in office cubicles a tenth of a second ago and, when you're 10, you were born .022 seconds ago.

A lot of time has passed before you and will likely pass after, unless this is but a dream, which we can't disprove.

Air

Your existence is temporary and fragile. Earth's

atmosphere is about 60 miles thick, but it doesn't have a fixed line; it just becomes thinner and thinner until it fades into space.[64] Despite this, most humans can only breathe and function well without supplemental oxygen up to about 2.27 miles (12,000 feet). This is the maximum altitude that the Federal Aviation Administration (FAA) allows pilots to fly without pressurized oxygen.[65]

According to the National Geographic Society, the highest city in the world is La Rinconada, Peru, in the Peruvian Andes. It's a gold-mining town that has about 30,000 inhabitants who live 3.16 miles (16,728 feet) above sea level without plumbing.

In celestial scales, 60 miles isn't much, and 3.16 miles is even less. The distance, for example, from Earth to the sun, which is a relatively close celestial body, is 92,960,000 miles. If these distances were proportional to the distance from Washington, D.C., to San Diego, so that the sun was in San Diego and you were standing in Washington, D.C., the atmosphere would only extend 7.74 feet out from Washington, and La Rinconada, the closest you could reasonably live unaided to San Diego, would only be 4.9 inches from where you are standing. You couldn't step beyond 4.9 inches toward the sun in San Diego without significant aid.

You can only live in a precariously thin sliver of vast space. Your survivability diminishes further if you include factors like food and water. You're only three missed meals away from becoming significantly uncomfortable. Try it. Thus, your habitable zone is about 3 miles up, 3 to 30 days out (without water and food), 3 minutes under water, and 0 to 130 degrees. Breach these boundaries for long; you die.

"Death is never very far."[66]

— Caliph Talib

Life is fragile as a wisp, and the universe doesn't care. We take life for granted and live like things are permanent, which is just as well, but they are not. Nothing is. Everything is just passing through in temporary states of consolidated energy.

Galaxies UGC 1810 and UGC 1813 collide. Gravitational forces rip galaxies apart and form new ones, tearing billions of stars, planets and solar systems asunder. Credit: NASA, ESA and the Hubble Heritage Team (STScl/AURA).[67]

Being-Space-Time

This gives you some perspective and helps geolocate you in being-space-time. Perspective matters. Leaders and happy people know where they are, where they are going, what is important and what is not. They're not aimlessly adrift, being perpetually pushed and pulled by social, professional and financial forces they can't see or control.

So the next time you become stressed, remember that you are 99 percent empty space, living on a speck of a speck of dust at an obscure outpost in a sliver of a sliver of time. Your problem isn't a problem to the universe, which could extinguish you with the slightest twitch. Worse has come before, and worse will come after, until it's all pulverized in cold cosmic death, one way or another. Statistically, statistics shouldn't exist, and someday you won't. But it does.

And you do.

Being-Space-Time-Consciousness

Looking inward, where are you consciously?

Daniel Tammet can calculate numbers in his head to 100 decimal places in a few seconds. He can speak 11 languages and once recited Pi (3.14 ...) to 22,514 decimal places in five hours and nine minutes, without error. To Tammet, each positive integer up to 10,000 has its own unique shape, color, texture and feel; 289 is ugly, 333 is attractive, Pi is beautiful, and 9 is large, towering and intimidating.[68,69] When he calculates, he sees pictures, shapes and patterns. "I'm seeing things in my head, like little sparks flying off, and it's not until the very last moment that those sparks tell me what on earth they mean."[70] Tammet calculates without seeming to think.

Steven "the Human Camera" Wiltshire can accurately draw complex images from memory. Once, he flew over London in a helicopter for 15 minutes and observed the city without using a camera or taking notes. He then sat at a 13-foot-long canvas and, over the course of five days, correctly drew seven square miles of London, down to the exact number of floors and windows on obscure buildings. One family friend said, "He does enter another world. Absolute stillness is the word I would use to describe Steven as he becomes the artist. He is just responding to something greater, beyond himself."[71]

Both Tammet and Wiltshire are savants. Unlike Tammet and Wiltshire, most savants have deep mental abilities in select areas, such as art, music or math, but struggle with day-to-day activities like social interaction or buttoning their shirts. They're blessed with superpowers and cursed with disabilities. Interestingly, many also suffer from brain damage to the left anterior temporal lobe.

Can you calculate like Tammet and draw like Wiltshire?

Most savants are born with their abilities. Some savant skills, however, can be suddenly acquired. When Orlando Serrell was 10, for example, a baseball hit him in the head. He lost consciousness. After he woke, he could calculate the day of week for any date in history. He can also instantly recall very specific details about events that occurred on days since his accident, like what he was doing, what he ate and what the weather was like. If, for example, you say, "February 11, 1983," he can tell you it was a Friday, it rained and he ate a Domino's pizza with sausage and pepperoni.[72] He does this instantly and effortlessly, without thinking. A few others also have this seemingly random "calendar calculator" skill. Serrell has no other savant skills, and works as a janitor.

The facts that savants are born with exceptional abilities (which they can empower further with brute practice), they seemingly perform similar feats without thinking, they frequently suffer from brain damage, and people can suddenly acquire savant skills from brain trauma, suggests that every brain has these abilities.

To test this, several studies tried to disable the conscious brain by bombarding it (in the left anterior temporal lobe) with magnets, a process called repetitive transcranial magnetic stimulation (rTMS). When scientists did this, some subjects drew, counted and solved problems better. Temporary "brain damage" made them smarter, and they replicated some savant skills.[73,74,75,76] It allowed them to access greater subconscious knowledge.

The Nine Dot Problem. Try connecting all nine dots, with four lines, without lifting your pen from the paper. The expected solution rate is 0 percent. Chi and Snyder asked 22 subjects to solve it. None did. They then impaired the subjects' conscious brain by zapping it with an rTMS-like procedure. Afterward, 40 percent solved it.[77] The solution is in Addendum B.

Studies like these, and people like Tammet, Wiltshire and Serrell, suggest that you have significantly more brainpower than you leverage, and that your subconscious captures a subterranean sea of detailed data. They suggest that your consciousness lays over this sea like a middle manager, and filters, processes and packages raw data into crude, manageable chunks so that you, the decision-making CEO, can interact, survive and propagate in a complicated macro landscape. Evolutionarily, this makes sense. Even though you, for example, can instantly divide 432 by 5 in your head subconsciously right now (you already know the answer – my calculator tells me it's 86.4), it doesn't help you run from a hyena; it hurts.

"The conscious mind may is a fountain playing in the sun and falling back into the great subterranean pool of subconscious from which it rises."[78]

— Sigmund Freud

Consciously assessing your conscious is "like trying to bite your own teeth,"[79] but if your brain is layered like this, do you retain memories of nearly everything you've ever seen, heard, felt, smelled and tasted? What are the implications of this?

"When an inner situation is not made conscious, it happens outside as fate."[80]

— Carl Jung

"Never repress anything."[81]

— Hampton

Given this, can we learn better? For the next 20 years, school will teach you to cram, repeat and memorize, so your monkey mind can fish minnows from your subconscious. They teach you these tactics because they work. But they're crude. Why do we need to repeat the Spanish word for to repeat (*repetir*) twenty times to know it, when may know it as soon as we've heard it once? Do you need to learn Spanish, or simply discover it? Don't cram, release. Get out of your own way. Let brilliance radiate up.

"He doesn't know where the music comes from, but it comes fully written. … 'It's as if the unconscious mind is giving orders at the speed of light … so I just hear it as if it were a smooth performance of a work that is already written, when it isn't."[82]

— 12-year-old music prodigy Jay Greenberg

Great ideas are frequently simple and obvious in retrospect. In fact, the best ideas are the simplest. Sometimes when you hear a great song for the first time, does it seem like you've already known it forever? Maybe these great ideas and songs have been transmitted so purely from the deep blue that they awaken the same chord already vibrating in you.

"Einstein once said that while Beethoven created his music, Mozart's was so pure that it seemed to have been ever-present in the universe, waiting to be discovered by the master. Einstein believed much the same of physics."[83]

— Arthur Miller

Einstein once said:

"At times I feel certain that I am right, while not knowing the reason."[84]

— Albert Einstein

Your conscious-subconscious synergy may be structured so that you can't gain something somewhere without losing something somewhere else. The brain needs to gist. You can't function if you're constantly distracted by detail. While Tammet, for example, speaks 11 languages, he has a hard time empathizing and communicating with people, and he can't drive, because he constantly processes distracting details he sees as he moves down the road.[85]

Conscious forgetting and ignorance aren't bad. If we didn't forget, we'd constantly relive pain. We'd spend our present living in our past. It's cathartic to let go, and sometimes the brain helps, even when we don't want it to.

But your brain is far vaster than your brain tells you it is. The world stretches far beyond the fish streams we swim, across the universe divide. Imagine the gogo girls we can't imagine. Qué diablos.

You're only confined by the walls you build. Kim Peek (the person *Rain Man* is based on), for example, could read two pages at once (one with each eye) in eight seconds, and recall them word for word years later. He could reportedly recall more than 12,000 books.[86] Even if this figure is exaggerated by 11,999 books, it's still impressive. Ramon Campayo can memorize 46 binary numbers in one second, which looks something like this:

1010111011000101010110101010110101001011010110

This can be done. It is done. And just like we've barely ventured outward in space and time, you've barely ventured inward into awareness. You've explored the jungle for years, yet hardly seen any of it. A raindrop falls for a thousand years. Come, come a little farther, because you're infinite.

You are Awareness.

In Presence.

X

PRESENCE

In late January 1968, Zenas M. was an Army Ranger in Vietnam. He was 25 years old and commanded 150 men. One day at base, a Search and Destroy (S&D) patrol radioed in that the VC had ambushed them. They were taking heavy fire and were pinned down. Zee and about 30 of his men jumped in helos to go extract and rescue them.

As they flew into the LZ, the VC were hitting Zee's Huey with so many bullets that "it sounded like someone was throwing gravel at a tin can." A tin can they were in.

The LZ was so hot that the pilots told Zee that they couldn't extract the platoon and had to RTB (return to base). Zee suddenly faced a tough choice. What decisions do most 25-year-olds have to make? Zee had to decide whether to leave his friends, men with families whose lives he was responsible for, to die, or to endanger himself and more men by dropping into the fight.

He didn't hesitate. He ordered the helos to drop them. "As soon as we left the helos, my guys started getting shot." The helos fled under heavy fire.

Zee's men hunkered into the grass with the other platoon and returned fire. Almost immediately, Zee realized that they were still outgunned, and now more men were pinned down.

Vietnam was not easy. In World War II, the average Army infantryman in the South Pacific experienced an average of 10 days of combat in a year. In Vietnam, the average infantryman experienced 240.[87]

That said, the average Marine in WWII in the South Pacific experienced constant combat. Your Great Grandpa JS (GGJS), for example, was a Marine Raider from 1939 to 1946. Island hopping toward Tokyo, he fought in New Caledonia, Espiritu Santo, Guadalcanal (which the Japanese called Starvation Island), Puruata Island, Savo Island, Bougainville, Emirau and Guam, among other places. After one battle, there were only two men still alive in his whole company. He was one of them. In his war notes, he said:

> "I preferred to be with the first wave on beach landings than in the tenth or fourteenth. Because of nerves and fear, your first shot is not as accurate as the ones that follow, and the same is true with the enemy on the beach."

On 21 July 1944, Japanese soldiers attacked a firebase that GGJS' platoon held on Guam. Like the VC attacking Zee, the Japanese had GGJS' men trapped. They charged GGJS' position all night until fewer and fewer Marines remained. Eventually, the Japanese began coming over the berms and jumping into Grandpa's bunker with ninja swords. It was hand-to-hand combat, and most of Grandpa's men were killed.

A few days later, the Japanese shot your Great Grandpa when his platoon attacked a pillbox in the jungle. He was put on a skiff that went down coast, collecting wounded Marines. On these skiffs, medics triaged the wounded.

They put wounded soldiers they assessed could be saved on a medical ship offshore. The medical ships, however, had limited space, so the medics had to leave soldiers who were wounded "beyond reasonable hope" on the skiffs.

As GGJS lay on the skiff, his neighbor from Connecticut happened to come by. His neighbor was a medic who was deciding whom to put on the medical ship. GGJS was too severely wounded to speak or open his eyes, but he heard his neighbor say, "I know that guy. That's [JS]. He won't make it." His neighbor decided not to send GGJS to the medical ship. He left him on the skiff to die.

In GGJS' neighbor's next letter home to his family in Connecticut, he noted that, "I saw [JS]. He was very nearly dead." The neighbor's family told GGJS' family this. Worried, GGJS' mom wrote the Secretary of the Navy and asked him what the status of her son was. GGJS had lost his dog tags and was too wounded to identify himself for a while. The Secretary of the Navy wrote GGJS' mom back and said that, unfortunately, he didn't know what the status of her son was.

At some point, the Marines filed a report that he'd been KIA. After a while, his family had a memorial service for him back home.

Your Great Grandpa, however, survived. The USS Hope medical ship came and took him. He recovered and eventually identified himself.

He believed that God saved him, and saved him for a reason, because he couldn't have survived WWII otherwise. Given this, he had a strong constitution. He believed in duty and sacrifice, and felt obligated to serve his family and community.

THE SECRETARY OF THE NAVY
WASHINGTON

The President of the United States takes pleasure
in presenting the SILVER STAR MEDAL to

FIRST LIEUTENANT JOHN L. STERLING,
UNITED STATES MARINE CORPS RESERVE,

for service as set forth in the following

CITATION:

"For conspicuous gallantry and intrepidity as
a Platoon Leader of Company K, Third Battalion, Fourth
Marines (Reinforced), First Provisional Marine Brigade,
Third Amphibious Corps, during action against enemy
Japanese forces on Guam, Marianas Islands, 21 July
1944. During repeated enemy counterattacks throughout the night, First Lieutenant Sterling skillfully
led his outnumbered forces in repulsing the enemy and
in inflicting severe losses although most of his men
were casualties before morning. Later in the campaign
in an assault against Japanese-held pillboxes, he
directed his men until he was seriously wounded. His
leadership and devotion to duty reflect the highest
credit upon First Lieutenant Sterling and the United
States Naval Service."

For the President,

Secretary of the Navy.

A few years later at Quantico, a commander called GGJS into his office and ordered him to wear his medals on base. GGJS didn't know what medals he had, and he'd never gotten any, so the commander sent a staff sergeant to look in his file. After a while, the staff sergeant returned and reported that GGJS' file said that he was dead. GGJS wrote:

> "I was at one time reported KIA. No report to the contrary was ever turned in. Some had one report, others had another. It just so happens that you are switched from one file to another, and in one, not much ever happens again."

GGJS had a good sense of humor.

Your Great Grandpa was awarded a Silver Star for Guam. For "conspicuous gallantry and intrepidity." He also had four Purple Hearts. A letter he wrote about discipline for you before he died is in Addendum C.

All four of your great grandfathers fought in, and survived, WWII.

Great Grandpa TH (GGTH) fought for the Air Force in Southeast Asia. He was an aircraft mechanic for the Flying Tigers in India and Burma.

Great Grandpa CP (GGCP) fought for the Navy in Europe and the South Pacific. He was an electronics technician on the USS Tulagi aircraft carrier, CVE-72. He fought in the invasion of Southern France (August 1944), the battle for Leyte Gulf in the Philippines (October 1944), the battle for Iwo Jima (February 1945) and the Invasion of Okinawa (April 1945). In his war notes he wrote:

> "Battle time was no picnic. There was always fear of some sort present. In the Mediterranean we feared plane attacks and buzz bombs. In the Pacific we feared the Japanese kamikazes. Submarines were always a threat.

> "One day, during the invasion of the Southern Philippines, we had sixteen aircraft carriers and about a hundred other ships, battleships, cruisers, destroyers, landing craft ... and there was one wave after another of kamikazes, about two hundred in the sky. ... Most of the time we'd shoot them down before they could attack the ship. ... [But] they sunk two ships, and two more got damaged. A kamikaze came for our ship, our aircraft carrier, and the bullets were so thick he couldn't

117

make it, so he veered off and he run into a cruiser, the St. Louis Cruiser I think was the name of it, and hit the bridge. Killed about fifteen people. All the officers who were up there got wiped out. ... War is not fun. It's a dangerous thing. But you just go to war to try to defend your country."

Great Grandpa DB (GGDB) fought for the Army in Europe. He was a Private First Class in the 607th Tank Destroyer Division, which was predominantly attached to the 82nd Airborne and the 90th infantry Divisions under General Patton. On D-day, 8 June 1944, your Great Grandpa landed on Utah Beach. In his war notes, he wrote:

"For as far as I could see there was nothing but ships of all kinds and sizes. As we got close to Normandy Beach there were a lot of American soldiers floating around the channel, all dead. The coastline was smoking from artillery and downed planes. ... The ship behind us hit a floating land mine, exploded and sank in five minutes."

Out of the 220 men in your Great Grandpa's company, 137 were killed. His tank, driving toward Berlin, fought in five of the seven major European battles: the Invasion of France, the Battle of the Bulge, St. Leo, Rhineland and Ardennes. His tank was credited with destroying one Tiger Tank, six Mark Fives, one Mark Four, six artillery trucks, two armored cars, seven half trucks and one horse-drawn cart. They knocked out 15 pillboxes and seven machine gun nests. GGDB estimated that he "killed between 150 and 200 Nazis."

Of the five guys in GGDB's tank, three were killed. He was nominated for a Silver Star and two bronze medals. He received the arrowhead for the Invasion of France, the

Bronze Star and a Purple Heart with two clusters.

Your great grandfathers fought for their country, and for their families.

Back in Vietnam, Zee and his men fought for hours. Many died. As their position weakened and their situation deteriorated, Zee became increasingly concerned that they would be overrun. The helos couldn't return, and they couldn't retreat. They were stuck.

By dusk, most of them were dead. The rest were scattered, exhausted and low on ammo. Then, Zee took a bullet in the ankle.

"I was out of ammunition. I had my knife out. Then I got shot. I knew that if the VC charged, they'd overrun us. I suddenly realized that I was going to die," he said.

"Once I realized this and accepted it, an incredible peace came over me. It was strange. It was like every worry I had and construct I'd propped up in my head for so long disintegrated. I no longer needed to hold them up. I no longer needed to worry about staying alive. It was like a relief. The peace was so vast. Everything was still. And I knew that it would all be okay. That's why I'm not afraid to die now. It was like touching the surface of a lake and making a single ripple."

His Ego, World View, Skandhas, Maya, Identity, Monkey Mind - whatever it is and whatever you want to call it - disintegrated, and he saw the world without judgement, ideas, history or time. He experienced it directly, as is, beautiful.

Shortly after, the VC stopped firing. Miraculously, they left. "We discovered later that they left to join the Tet

Offensive. If they would have charged, they would have killed the rest of us."

Zee lived. Forty-five years later, he said that no matter what he has done since and no matter how hard he has meditated or tried, he has never been able to replicate the stillness and clarity of that moment. That Presence.

After Vietnam, Zee became a psychologist. He theorized that one reason vets experience Post Traumatic Stress Disorder (PTSD) is because combat is so intense that it dissolves space and time and rips them into the present, into presence.

Once vets return home, the past, future, ego and monkey mind return, intensified by expansion, and they're depressed that they can't escape this fog and recreate that presence.

XI

TRANSCEND

None but ourselves can free our minds.

— Bob Marley

Where is this presence and flow in you? How do you touch the void without dying in combat?

Here's a conception:

Everything consists of the same base matter: energy. You, the sun, a tree, water, the topography of the universe, everything: energy.

Energy can't be created or destroyed, only converted into different forms. Energy is mass and light, and mass and light are energy. In physics, this is captured in Einstein's equation: Energy equals mass times the speed of light squared; $E=mc^2$.

Small objects contain tremendous energy. A paper clip, for example, contains the same amount of energy as the atomic bomb that destroyed Hiroshima in 1945.[88] That is, if you can convert all the mass in a paper clip into its energy, you can destroy a large city. With a paper clip.

Our minds perceive energy at a crude, macro wavelength. They filter, dull and de-amplify the intensity and depth of singularities to manage multiple objects over time, which optimizes survival.

A filter screens us from the world. A thought tornado encircles us that consists of our ego, identity, mind, judgement, assumption, categorization, emotions, physical cravings, past, future …

When we dilute or punch through this filter we see the raw world as is. As beautiful light and infinite energy. Colors brighten and sounds layer. Objects stretch and connect. Calculations collapse and truths surface. There is peace and clarity.

When you're awareness rests in this moment, you're present. When you surf the mind and universe, you flow. You don't think, you don't calculate, because you don't need to, you just know.

The universe is always like this, even now, as you read this, it's vibrating fluid around you, like infrared rays you can't see, or the stream around the trout. If we could see it, we'd be too distracted by minutia to function over time, like Tammet is too captivated by detail to drive.

Some savants and autistics may have damaged filters, which let them see deep and narrow instead of shallow and wide. They struggle to capture and transmit this technicolor depth to the dull grey working level, like most struggle to escape monkey mind multitasking to see the vast raw world beyond the stream. Those that can navigate between these worlds, like Van Gogh, Mozart and Newton, are explorers and translators who snatch pearls from the depths.

How can we breach our filters to experience other wavelengths?

First, realize that infinity is your base state. You don't need to add anything. You need to subtract it. Subtract Thought, Want, Fear, control, anger and resistance. Don't become. Un-become, because you're perfect as you are.

"We spend our whole lives trying to become who we already are."

— Unattributed

One day a young Buddhist on his journey home came to the banks of a wide river. Staring hopelessly at the great obstacle in front of him, he pondered for hours on how to cross such a wide barrier.

As he was about to give up, he saw a great Zen master on the other side. "Master," the young Buddhist yelled, "can you tell me how to get to the other side of this river?"

The Zen master looked up and down the river and pondered for a moment. Then he yelled back, "My son, you are on the other side of the river."

Second, don't overestimate presence. It isn't permanent and you've experienced it before. Monks experience it when they meditate. Athletes experience it in the zone. You may experience it on a walk in the woods. It comes and goes to varying degrees and you can't always live in it. Hunger pulls you back into your tactical mind. So don't seek a mythical nirvana that doesn't exist.

Spoon Boy: "Do not try and bend the spoon. That's impossible. Instead … only try to realize the truth."

Neo: "What truth?"

Spoon Boy: "There is no spoon."

Neo: "There is no spoon?"

Spoon Boy: "Then you'll see, that it is not the spoon that bends, it is only yourself."[89]

— *The Matrix*, Wachowski & Wachowski

Third, you don't need combat to access presence, because the universe surrounds you, always. One reason people summit peaks, walk on wires, race cars, defuse bombs and get drunk is to escape thought and muscle awareness into the present. Think about this: We have to stick our head in a lion's mouth to fully experience a present moment that we're already living in. That's crazy. We're comatose. We know it and can't wake up.

"The only Zen you find on top of mountains is the

Zen you bring up there."[90]

— Robert Pirsig

But we can wake up. You can enjoy presence and flow by managing energy, clearing the mind, aiming awareness, entering the now and letting go.

Manage Energy

Working inward, first, manage the energy around you. If everything is energy that can't be destroyed, only transformed, are you, in some remote way, energetically connected with everything?

"But I'll tell you what hermits realize. If you go off into a far, far forest and get very quiet, you'll come to understand that you are connected to everything."

— Alan Watts

Connect to positive energy. Some people are positive. Some aren't. The positive enrich you. The negative limit you.

"All matter is merely energy condensed to a slow vibration ... we are all one consciousness experiencing itself subjectively. There is no such thing as death; life is only a dream, and we are the imagination of ourselves. Here's Tom with the weather."[91]

— Bill Hicks

Ignore bullies, obstructionists, critics, destroyers and emotional vampires. They create unhappiness. Find healers and creators.

All of you are natural empaths. You're sensitive to people's energy, and have naturally high social and emotional intelligence. This is like a spider-sense superpower. Know when to activate and deactivate it. Some people, for example, are so sensitive that if someone is depressed, they become depressed. Others are so insensitive that they murder people. If you feel bad for every handicapé in Congo, you'll be miserable. But connect with some periodically, because this is humanity.

When energy crashes into you, respond rather than react. A car cuts you off, you feel mad. You get a good parking space, you're happy. We blindly react to whatever we happen to bump into. We bump around, and our happiness is determined by random external events. Ignore the guy who cuts you off. Enjoy the parking space.

There are a lot of bad people in the world doing bad things. They should be stopped. This is important. But destroying evil is destructive, and it's an ugly job. When you play with shit, you get shit on you. Do your duty, but when you're done and tired destroying evil, regenerate yourself by creating good.

Clear the Mind

"Empty your mind, be formless, shapeless — like water. Now you put water in a cup, it becomes the cup. You put water into a bottle, it becomes the bottle. You put it in a teapot, it becomes the teapot. Now water can flow or it can crash. Be water, my friend."[92]

— Bruce Lee

As detailed, drop things and declutter. Drop any useless Want, Fear, Identity, anger, anxiety, control and attachment. These can infect the mind and limit happiness. Clean your mind like you clean your room. What does your closet look like? Does your mind look like this?

Aim Awareness

The stronger your Awareness becomes, the more you can do, and the less other people, thoughts and circumstances can influence and imprison you. Your Awareness is like a spotlight. Whatever you focus it on you see, reveal, energize and grow, like a flashlight in a cave, or sunlight on a plant. Whatever you focus on increases.

If you worry about deadlines, you'll create more deadlines (and worry more). If someone betrays and hurts you and you keep thinking about it, it keeps hurting you. If you wonder what space is expanding into, you may learn more about cosmology.

Put your awareness and energy into injustice, hate, ambition, creativity or happiness, and you'll find more injustice, hate, ambition, creativity or happiness. Anything. Try it. Take something random, like the number 33. Write it on a notecard, look at it every morning when you wake up for a week and see if you see the number 33 more.

Even simpler, go look at a tree in your yard. You'll see ridges, textures and colors that you've never noticed before, simply because you're looking at them.

If you're not taking an objective, like learning a language or running a fast mile, as quickly as you like, unless you are at your physical limit, you may not be putting enough awareness on it. If you're not putting enough awareness on target, ask yourself why. Is half your Awareness running with the Monkey, distracted by pseudo problems? If you're going to worry about something, ensure it's worth worrying about.

The world gives you what you give it, and whatever you focus on, you see. That's all. Physically put your Awareness where you want it. Control what you turn your head to look at. Your Awareness surfaces preexisting truths, which is another way that you create your own reality.

"Whatever a monk keeps pursuing with his thinking and pondering, that becomes the inclination of his awareness."[93]

— Buddha

This is usually paraphrased as:

"What you think, you become."

Enter the Now

Once you manage the energy in your macro environment, clear your mind and control your awareness spotlight, enter the now.

What are some of the happiest times of your life? Were they moments, or memories of moments?

Presence and flow are experienced in the present. Not in the past or future, but in the now. In this very moment. The past and future are concepts of the mind that may not exist beyond the mind. Time is not as ridged as imagined.

"I was sitting in a chair in the patent office at Bern when all of sudden a thought occurred to me: If a person falls freely, he will not feel his own weight. I was startled. This simple thought made a deep impression on me."[94]

— Albert Einstein

Einstein said that this thought impelled him toward a theory of relativity, which showed, among other things, that gravity and velocity bend space-time.[95] This means, for example, that if one twin went into space, traveled at 99.9 percent the speed of light and returned five years later, he would be five years older, while the twin who remained on earth would be 110 years older. Time is relative to the observer. It is, flexible.

At the end of this paragraph, stop for a minute. Take a deep breath, close your eyes and let your mind run. Let it wander wherever it wants. Follow your thoughts wherever they lead. One after the next. After a minute, stop and jot down your thoughts.

What thoughts did you have? How many were there? Where did they take you? Did you start thinking about thinking, and end up thinking about why Band-Aid wrappers never fall in the garbage can, why we can't un-push elevator buttons or how blind people find the braille sign on ATMs to begin with? How many thoughts were about the past? The future? The present?

This is your normal, default operating mode. Your Monkey, always thinking and chasing. Frequently living in the past or future.

Now, at the end of this paragraph, stop for another minute and worry. Worry as much as you want. Enjoy it. After a minute, jot down what you worried about. Go.

What did you worry about? How many of these

problems were problems you had in the past? How many were problems you may have in the future? How many were problems that you have right now, in this very present? Any?

We rarely have problems in the now, like having someone yell or shoot at us. Are the chirping birds causing you problems? The sun? Wind? We import problems from the past and future like cargo and drape them over the now like a wet blanket. The bully only makes fun of you once, but you can feel it a hundred times — if you let it. And that's your choice. He only hurt you once. You let him hurt you a hundred times. Relatively few moments, few unfiltered nows, comprise the entirety of our thoughts and lives.

Now, at the end of this paragraph, stop again for a minute. Look up from the words. Close your eyes and breathe. Feel the sun on your skin and the wind in your hair. Smell the salt of the ocean, listen to the birds, hear the sound of the leaves. You will have thoughts. Let them come and go. Don't chase them like before. Watch them pass in front of you, like you're watching water from behind a waterfall. Just keep returning to breath, sounds, smells and feeling. Let go. Surrender. Feel energy flow up and down through your core and limbs. This is the now. This is Presence. This is the universe, flowing through you.

"The future is a concept — it doesn't exist. There is no such thing as tomorrow. There never will be, because time is always now. That's one of the things we discover when we stop talking to ourselves and stop thinking. We find there is only present, only an eternal now."

— Alan Watts

"Life is now. There was never a time when your life was not now, nor will there ever be."[96]

— Eckhart Tolle

Even though life is always now, we usually don't live in it. We spend much of our lives, many of our nows, living in the past, or imagining and living in the future. Around 600 BC, the Chinese Tao master Laozi wrote:

"If you are depressed, you are living in the past. If you are anxious, you are living in the future. If you are at peace, you are living in the present."[97]

Twelve hundred years later, in 600 AD, the following statement is attributed to the fourth Sunni Caliph, Ali Ibn Abi Talib, who was the Muslim prophet Muhammad's cousin:

"How strange and foolish is man ... he ruins his present while worrying about his future, but weeps in the future by recalling his past."

The now is frequently only a means to an end, a means to get to an imagined future point of increased happiness. Tolle articulated this well in "The Power of Now," which is frequently cited here. Once we get promoted, get a car, get a spouse ... once we reach a happiness milestone, the payout quickly fades, and we set another happiness milestone. We qualify happiness. But do we have to? Do we need something to be happy, after establishing basic comforts and biological balance?

"Stress is caused by being here but wanting to be there."[98]

— Eckhart Tolle

The past and future are ideas that exist in the mind, unless imported into the present. The future may manifest itself as imagined; it may not. And once the past is lived, is it just a story?

"Now is the only point that can take you beyond the limited confines of the mind. It is your only point of access into the timeless and formless realm of Being."[99]

— Eckhart Tolle

"Amelie has a strange feeling of absolute harmony. It's a perfect moment. Soft light, a scent in the air, the quiet murmur of the city … she breathes deeply. Life is simple and clear."[100]

— *Amelie*, Laurant & Jeunet

When were you so engaged and engrossed in something that time flew by? That you didn't notice it? A hike, a football game, playing? These moments are so raw and enjoyable, and the past and future can be so heavy, and the Monkey so clamorous, that people strive to recreate them.

The older you get, the bigger your Monkey gets; the more past and future you'll experience, create and carry; and the less you'll play.

"Children have neither a past nor a future. Thus they enjoy the present, which seldom happens to us."[101]

— Bruyère

That said, kids also crap themselves. Just yesterday, in the span of a minute, Little Bear pulled his peanuts out halfway across the room as he was running to the toilet so he could go faster, and Kidogo actually tried to pick his nose with my finger.

Regardless, as we age, we create the concept of a future and manipulate the now to produce more happiness in the future. Good. Do this. It works. It helps optimize happiness over time in the happy hunt. But don't continually work and worry for a future that never comes. Periodically cash in your work and enjoy the dividends. Work hard, play hard, and the harder you work, the harder you can play.

> "So I recommend having fun, because there is nothing better for people in this world than to eat, drink and enjoy life. That way they will experience some happiness along with all the hard work God gives them under the sun."

> — Ecclesiastes 8:15

From time to time, stop time. Shed Identity, forget the past, dissolve the future, cage the Monkey and breathe. A couple of times a day, watch the rain, feel the sun and hear the wind to re-center and regenerate yourself. If you drop Identity, past, future and negative Thoughts, you'll drop problems, and can enjoy underlying presence.

> "The music is not in the notes, but in the silence between."

> — Wolfgang Amadeus Mozart

In unfiltered presence and synchronicity, the now is an enjoyable end unto itself. But in the filtered mind world, the now isn't always enjoyable. When you're in football camp, 23 miles into a marathon or studying for a test, the now is painful. Then, it can help to escape the filtered now and live in the future. You have to imagine yourself being an Olympian to surmount the pain of becoming one.

In the day to day working now, you can also amplify the now by adding the past. Remembering Kidogo in his leisure suit in Kenya still makes me laugh, even now. Dancing with Pips at her wedding will be even more enjoyable when I remember her dancing on my feet in Washington.

You can lay the past and future over the present like GPS layers. Sometimes this worsens the now, sometimes it improves it. When you do, you experience the now indirectly, through time filters.

"As I ran outside to tell the children, I'm suddenly overcome with the shear, simple beauty of the day. It was as if I spent the last year seeing the world through a dark grey veil, and now, finally, that grey is gone."

— Anne Purcell, upon learning her husband, who was MIA for a year in Vietnam, was possibly alive in a POW camp

Mentally travel to whatever point in time provides the most happiness. When the filtered now is painful, jump to the future and live it through an idea in your ideosphere. When the past and future are painful, return to the unfiltered raw now. Time travel, knowing that the unfiltered now is simple, clear and luminous.

Two tactics to penetrate your filter, escape the mind world and put awareness in the now are meditation and mindfulness.

Meditating

Studies indicate that meditation can increase empathy, awareness, peace and happiness. It can release opioids and physically rewire your brain to be happier.[102]

"Meditation is not a way of making the mind quiet. It's a way of entering into the quiet that's already there, buried under the 50,000 thoughts the average person thinks every day."

— Deepak Chopra

You've already meditated. You did this when you closed your eyes, breathed and listened to the birds. That's it. Simple. You don't have to go to a temple in Tibet, and there's nothing complicated about it. Don't expect the heavens to split. Don't expect anything. Don't go to peace like you go to war. Just release expectation and let it be.

Fix yourself in the present and tell yourself that everything is okay. Every noise and itch is okay. In fact they're good, because they're keeping your Awareness fixed in the present. You're setting aside your Monkey and problems for a few minutes to focus on the world. To just look at the universe.

"The more we try to catch hold of the present moment, the more elusive it becomes. It is like trying to clutch water in one's hands. The harder we grip, the more it slips through our fingers."

— Alan Watts

Meditate like you do push-ups. Exercise Awareness like you exercise a muscle.

Mindfulness

Mindfulness is being mindful of the present without judgment. Like meditation, it helps you control your awareness and focus it on what you want to focus it on, instead of letting it be kidnapped by the Monkey, Narco, thoughts, depression, ads and other monkeys.

Take something you do every day, like walking across a gravel yard. Every day, before you start across the yard, tell your Monkey to set its problems and thoughts aside while you walk across the yard. Don't worry, they'll be waiting for you on the other side.

As you walk, focus on the act of walking. Notice sights, sounds, smells and feelings. Watch your steps, hear the CRUNCH of gravel, see the space between the rocks, feel the sun on your skin. Just observe the present. The world.

You can do this with any activity and it only takes a minute. Do it every time you walk home from the gym, get in your car for work, walk to the mailbox or jog. When you do it every day, you'll be surprised to see how constantly consumed your mind is with thoughts and problems. Every day when you come to edge of the yard, for example, see if your mind is subconsciously working on a different problem, and see if it is surprisingly hard to disengage from that problem even for a minute while you walk across the yard.

This simple exercise can increase appreciation, relaxation and happiness. It releases opioids, and researchers have used it to break drug addictions.[103]

Can you see the world without judgment? Not all the time, or even for a day, but just for a minute. A single minute. Can you? It's harder than you think to see a tree.

Other Tactics

Like meditation, you can use hypnosis to explore consciousness and sub-consciousness. Depending on how meditation and hypnosis are defined and used, both surpass the conscious mind filter, but meditation tends to focus more on sensing the subconscious, while hypnosis focuses more on changing it. Both tactics, however, can increase awareness and mind-control.

You need the Monkey to solve fixed-logic problems, but it helps to distract it to access deep creativity. Meditation, mindfulness and hypnosis can do this. But so can other activities that produce similar brain states, like walking, driving, hiking, sleeping, knitting, doing Legos, drawing, taking a shower or shooting baskets. Simple, repetitive activities like these are soothing, because they focus the Monkey on deconstructing the activity, rather than deconstructing you.

Shooting baskets, for example, forces the Monkey to focus on dribbling and shooting. These tasks are complicated enough that they engage the Monkey, but simple enough that your awareness can slip away and watch the subconscious surface.

What activities soothe you? Are they repetitive, slightly engaging activities that free your subconscious?

When do you have your best ideas? When Thomas Edison was stuck on a problem, he would reportedly take a nap and allow his subconscious to work on it. Friedrich August Kekule von Stradonitz said that the ring structure of benzene came to him in a dream, when he dreamt about a snake eating its own tail.[104] He already knew the answer subconsciously; he just had to kick his Monkey off it.

The same thing happens when something is on the tip of your tongue. You can't recall the answer, but you know that you know it. How can you not know something, but know that you know it?

"When I am traveling in a carriage, or walking after a good meal, or during the night when I cannot sleep, it is on such occasions that ideas flow best and most abundantly."

— Wolfgang Amadeus Mozart

A study found that over 60 percent of test subjects who played Tetris during the day dreamt about playing it at night. The mind continued to work on the problem during sleep.[105] Try giving your Monkey a constructive problem and telling him to work on it while you sleep.

Another Tetris study found, counter intuitively, that the harder each level becomes, the less brainpower you spend on it.[106] That is, the more often you do something, the stronger a neural path you build and the easier it becomes. Given this, the more constructive thought trails you walk, the easier they are to relocate and stroll. The more you focus on happiness, the happier you can be. You can train your brain to do positive feedback loops.

Let Go

The world is. Refusing to accept this creates unhappiness.

"What screws us up more, life or the picture in our head about how life is supposed to be?"

— Unattributed

The world is yours for the taking. Actively engage it, improve it and fight like a badger when needed, but do it consciously. Accept new circumstances, then advance on a positive bearing. Engage the world like Judo, flowing with it like water and using its momentum against itself. Let it come to you.

"The world is already yours. Why try to conquer it?"

— Rasheed Ogunlaru

Decide when to fight and when to accept. What you fight you focus on, and what you focus on increases, so allocate your limited awareness to worthy fights, then crush them completely. When you fight something, you don't dominate it, you submit to it. You only dominate it once you've conquered and forgotten it completely. Until then, it owns part of your mind.

"The meaning of life is just to be alive. It's so plain and so obvious and so simple. And yet, everyone rushes around in a great panic as if it were necessary to achieve something beyond themselves."

— Alan Watts

Once, I was about to come home after being gone for several months. The day before returning, I talked to Little Bear on the phone. He was four at the time. "Heh bud," I said, "what do you want to do when I get home?"

"Furst," He said, in his strange Boston accent that nobody knows where he got it from, "I'm gonna give you a hug. Then I'm gonna give ya a gut check. Then I'm gonna take ya to Five Guys."

I laughed. The kid had a plan.

"Ya, that sounds like a good day Bear. A real good day."

And it was.

After eating hamburgers with you back home, I sat on a bench with Mom in the park and watched you guys play. There was meat in my stomach and sun on my skin. The leaves flickered and you guys laughed. Sparkled. I smiled and asked myself, "What more do I need?"

This is happiness to a father and a husband.

Accept and enjoy.

A long time ago, there was a great Zen master named Banzan. Banzan spent many years meditating, trying to become enlightened. Enlightenment, however, failed him.

One day, Banzan was walking though the market, and he overheard a conversation between a butcher and his customer.

"Give me the best piece of meat you have," the customer said.

"Every piece of meat I have is the best," the butcher said. "There is no piece of meat that is not the best piece of meat."

Upon hearing this, Banzan became enlightened.[107]

XII

BLEEDING OUT

The other day, in Iraq, a translator and I were talking on the phone to a Yazidi grandmother. She had been trapped on Sinjar Mountain and had come down the mountain with her three granddaughters to try to get food from a village at the base of the mountain. Islamic State of Iraq and the Levant (ISIL) jihadists, however, were attacking the village with DShKs and uparmored American Humvees. She and her granddaughters were pinned down by gunfire.

"What should I do?" She asked.

"Get out of there," I said.

"I can't. I can't leave my son."

"Where's he?"

"In the village, fighting."

"How old is he?"

"Twenty-six."

"Forget him. You have to leave him. He's old enough to take care of himself. You can't help him. But you can help your granddaughters. Think about them. Protect them and go back up the mountain."

"I can't. The oldest girl, her feet are bloody. The second one is too tired and won't move, and the baby is strapped to my back."

"Where are you?"

"Between some rocks. There are dead bodies all around. Dash [ISIL] is shooting everything."

"What's the name of the village?"

"I don't know."

"Do you have any water?"

"No, but we found a dead duck this morning."

The translator waited for her to finish speaking.

"She said that they ate it raw," the translator relayed.

"Can you help us?" she asked.

We couldn't help them. We didn't know where they were and ISIL was closing on our position. What do you tell someone in a situation like that?

A few days before, ISIL had overrun Sinjar. Sinjar wasn't supposed to fall. The Kurds were protecting it. They had Peshmerga troops there but lacked heavy weapons and air assets, so they had to reach, supply and defend Sinjar by driving south from Faysh Khabur, Kurdistan.

The Kurds controlled the road from Faysh Khabur to Sinjar, but it ran 60 miles along the Syria-Iraq border. It was riddled with IEDs and bordered by Arab tribes with shifting loyalties. The Kurds didn't control anything beyond the range of an AK on either side of the road, or anything around Sinjar. They held a thin umbilical cord to an isolated outpost in Indian country. ISIL had them surrounded, and ISIL wanted Sinjar. They wanted to blow through it, eradicate resistance and establish direct contact with their territory in northern Syria.

Sinjar, the Yazidis who lived there and the Kurdish Peshmerga were dangerously exposed. The Kurds, however, had vowed to defend Sinjar and their Yazidi cousins with their lives.

The Yazidis say that foreign forces have attacked and tried to annihilate them 72 times in history. The Yazidis are surrounded by Sunni and Shi'a Arabs who consider them devil worshippers, because one of the seven angels they worship, or appease, Melek Taus, is a fallen angel like Satan. The Yazidis now faced a 73rd genocide.

The Kurds thought Sinjar would hold, because up until that point the Kurds had been the only thing that had stopped ISIL. ISIL had conquered and killed everyone else. When ISIL took Mosul a few months before, in early June 2014, after rotting it for months from the inside like mold, the Iraqi Army stripped off their uniforms and fled.

In early August 2014, ISIL attacked Sinjar and overran it like a brush fire, despite the Kurds' brave stand. The U.S. had not authorized airstrikes, so the Kurds were on their own. The U.S. had supported the Kurds for years, but simultaneously starved them with the One-Iraq policy. Under "One-Iraq," all of America's weapons went to the One-Iraqis in Baghdad. None went to the One-Iraqis in

Kurdistan. The Arab Iraqis thus had American ammunition, heavy weapons, uparmored Humvees and Abrams tanks, while the Kurdish Iraqis had old AK47s and a few tanks that they'd taken from Saddam. When the Iraqi Army fled, they left these American weapons, ammunition and equipment for ISIL. ISIL got five Army divisions of American weapons.

Kurdish officials, in meetings, frequently noted that not only had the U.S. not given them any weapons, but the Kurds were now, absurdly, actually fighting against American weapons that ISIL had and being killed by them.

Given this, the Peshmerga were outgunned and outmatched. The Arab tribes in Sinjar had also secretly worked with ISIL and venomously betrayed their Yazidi neighbors, letting ISIL in the backdoor at night, then stealing the Yazidis' things after ISIL sliced their throats.

ISIL came into Sinjar shooting. Some Yazidis stayed in Sinjar town, while others took their chances on Sinjar Mountain, like they'd done for centuries. ISIL killed all the Yazidi men who stayed and enslaved the women. They raped wives, daughters and girls, and buried and burnt people alive. This didn't happen 2,000 years ago. It happened a few months ago.

ISIL tried to push up Sinjar Mountain but were rebuffed by a small, heroic force of Yazidi men armed with AKs, steep terrain and motivation. Motivation to live.

Sinjar "Mountain", however, barely qualifies as a mountain. It's a barren rock with no food and limited water. The Yazidis believe it was the final resting place for Noah's Ark.

Between 20,000 and 50,000 Yazidis fled up the

mountain, and ISIL knew that they could simply starve them out and kill them as they came down. Meanwhile, for fun, ISIL shot them with sniper rifles on the mountain. The Yazidis' AKs didn't have enough range, or ammo, to effectively fire back.

As the days passed, Yazidis starved. Grandparents and babies died, especially as the mothers, who didn't have food or much water, stopped producing milk. Some Yazidis tried to sneak off the mountain to escape to Syria. It's bad when you want to escape to Syria. Others believed ISIL's promise that ISIL wouldn't harm them if they came down, so they did. ISIL enslaved and beheaded them.

"What should I do?" The grandmother asked again, trapped in heavy crossfire near the village at the foot of Sinjar mountain.

The translator could hear gunfire in the background, but her granddaughters no longer cried.

"Tell her we're trying," I said. "Stay focused on your granddaughters, and survive."

This was a flat, useless response. She couldn't do anything with it. She couldn't drink it. She couldn't eat it. She couldn't kill with it. It was all I had.

After we hung up, the translator and I looked at each other silently. A heavy thought hung in the air. They were going to die. And almost all we could do, was hang up.

Losing Sinjar dealt a significant psychological blow to the Kurds. They had withstood ISIL for months, while the heavily armed Iraqi Army evaporated in their underwear, then lost Sinjar in two days. In Kurdish, Peshmerga means "those who seek death." Death had found them.

Death is near, when people are bone scared.

On 6 August 2014, an ISIL mortar hit a Kurdish platoon in a bunker on the front between Mosul and Kurdistan. The mortar killed the Peshmerga platoon commander. The remaining Peshmerga called Command and asked to be relieved. Their post was the farthest post south, just a few miles north of Mosul. They had been defending it for weeks. They hadn't slept in four days, they were out of ammo and their commander had just died.

Command, however, didn't have any Peshmerga left to relieve them. The Kurds were defending a hostile border 1,100 kilometers long that ran from Syria to Iran.

After Command told the soldiers that they had to stay in their post, the soldiers discussed their situation. They were exhausted, thirsty and hungry. They didn't have any ammunition, and they knew that if ISIL advanced, in a gust of wind, they would die. Given this, they decided to tactically retreat to the next post, away from Mosul, toward Kurdistan.

When the platoon walked into the next post north, the captain of that post asked them what the hell they were doing and why they'd left their post. After the platoon explained their situation, the larger post realized that they faced similar circumstances. Their post was now the front, and they couldn't defend it. Given this, they also decided to fall back to the next post north. When the next post saw their two forward posts had retreated, they did too.

This retreat, whose tipping point occurred from a single mortar, triggered a chain reaction. Kurdish forces across the Mosul front retreated. They left silently in the middle of the night, trying not to alert the local villages they had been protecting. The villagers, however, soon realized what was happening. Fear and panic spread, as fear and panic do, and the villagers followed the soldiers.

Within hours, a biblical wave of humanity flooded north. ISIL advanced, and the Kurds fled to their mountains near Turkey, like they did when Saddam gassed them. The Kurds would sleep in the hills like animals and become guerrillas again. ISIL could loot the cities, but if ISIL fought them in the mountains, ISIL would suffer. As said, "The Kurds have no friends but the mountains."

As the Kurdish front collapsed and ISIL advanced, they closed on our position.

After hanging up with the grandmother, my boss and I called a local friend who was supposed to help protect us.

"Can you protect us?" He asked.

When reinforcements ask if you can reinforce them, it could be better. I didn't respond.

"Are we getting airstrikes?" He said, "Or should I make alternative plans?"

I clenched my jaw and rubbed my head. His world was disintegrating, and we could only give him the truth. "You should make alternative plans." I said.

There was a long, loud silence. His breath was uneven. His voice trembled. He was exhausted, and that nearly broke him. "Okay," he said, bravely, "Take care of my family."

We evacuated most our personnel in an airlift. We were busy and hadn't slept much. But between calls and cables I wrote a text message to you. I saved it as draft so that all I had to do was hit send if the situation deteriorated.

Instead of writing a text message, I wanted to send you this field guide, but at the time it was mostly just a disorganized list of bullet points and half-thoughts from your Buddha books. So I basically had to write this entire field guide in one minute, in a text message. I had to condense everything I wanted to teach and tell you in your entire lives into a few sentences. What would you say?

Shortly after I drafted the SMS, America authorized airstrikes. The President authorized airdrops on Sinjar Mountain and airstrikes on ISIL.

F18s seared the sky, severing it like paper and dropping death. Booming, deafening death. Death that shook the earth. ISIL felt the full reach and force of American power.

The airstrikes saved Kurdistan, and the airdrops saved Yazidis. When innocent people needed help, America was there.

The airstrikes blunted ISIL and secured our position.

A few days later, as I was walking to do burpees, the translator fell into stride beside me.

"Heh," he said, "our grandma called."

"What?"

"Ya, she lived. She and her granddaughters survived."

I stared, amazed.

"Ya. She called to say thanks. She said that shortly after

she hung up, airplanes came out of the sky and fired at the Humvees." Like angels.

Slowly, I smiled.

Grandmother and her three granddaughters escaped Sinjar Mountain. They traveled to Syria, and crossed back into Kurdistan through Faysh Khabur. They were safe and healthy, amongst the noble Kurds.

After things calmed down, I looked at the draft text message again. The one piece of advice I decided to give you when pressured, of all the advice in this world and this guide, bleed out to two sentences for Mom, and four words for you. That is, if you only remember one thing from this guide, remember this:

"We've passed a hundred thousand miles. Tell my wife I love her very much, she knows. Boo, Kidogo, Little Bear and Pips: Have kids, like me. Love, Dad"

Addendum A

A graphic on the happy hunt happiness process. Keep in mind that I just made this up. A professor once told my class, "Half of what I'm about to tell you is wrong. I just don't know which half."

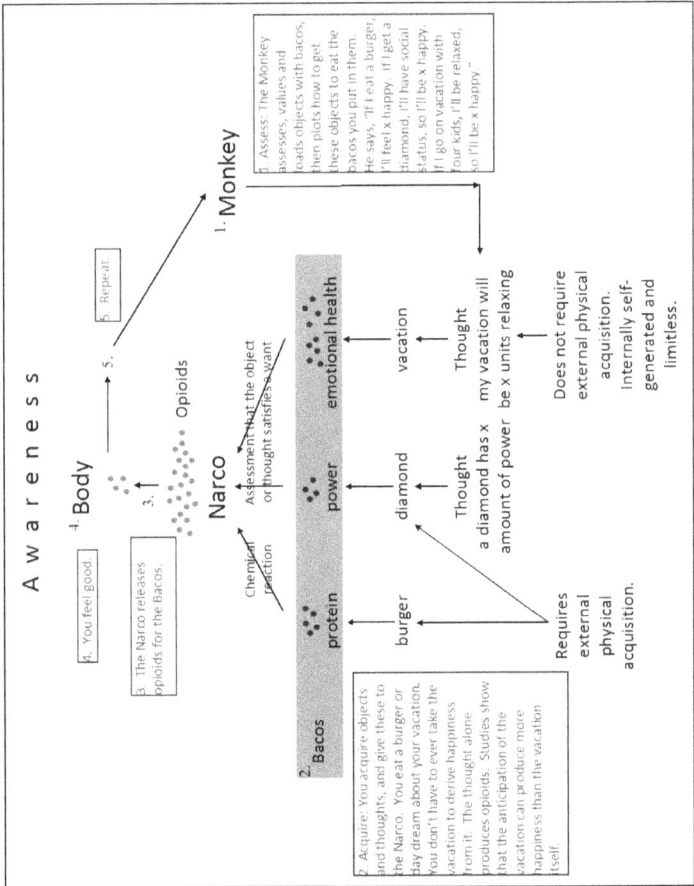

A w a r e n e s s

⁴ Body

¹· Monkey

1. Assess: The Monkey assesses, values, and loads objects with bacos, then plots how to get these objects to eat the bacos you put in them. He says, "If I eat a burger, I'll feel x happy. If I get a diamond, I'll have social status, so I'll be x happy. If I go on vacation with your kids, I'll be relaxed, so I'll be x happy."

5. Repeat.

5.

Opioids

3.

Narco

Assessment that the object or thought satisfies a want

Chemical reaction

4. You feel good.

3. The Narco releases opioids for the Bacos.

² Bacos	protein	power	emotional health

| burger | diamond | vacation |

| Thought a diamond has x amount of power | Thought my vacation will be x units relaxing |

Requires external physical acquisition.

Does not require external physical acquisition. Internally self-generated and limitless.

2. Acquire: You acquire objects and thoughts, and give these to the Narco. You eat a burger or day dream about your vacation. You don't have to ever take the vacation to derive happiness from it. The thought alone produces opioids. Studies show that the anticipation of the vacation can produce more happiness than the vacation itself.

Addendum B

The solution to the nine dot problem.

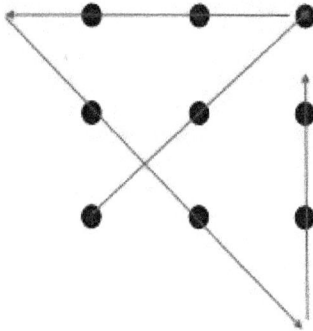

Addendum C

A letter from your Great Grandpa.

#2.

Like It Or Not-You Have to Have It!
By   Grandpa

We were never allowed to use the word "hate" in our family. But, as with all kids and a lot of grown-ups, I had to indure discipline. Yes, and we all disliked it! Make your bed, clean your room, be home by 10 pm, stop this and stop that are part of growing up. You get discipline at school,at work, in sports and then you get married and discipline will not go away. I shouldn't say it but I hated discipline!

Before I tell you a short story, let me tell you that the true definition of discipline can not be found in the dictionary nor is it very often defined to you by your parents. The truth is that discipline is the closest word to love that I know of-it is not only a sign of love but it is love. The big thing about discipline is that it leads to self-discipline. You know, all those little things like brushing your teeth, saying please, thank you, being courteous and polite, and phone calls and cards even though, at the time, you do not realize just how important they are.

I was born into a strict Episcopalian, Conneticut family. "Thou shall not kill, Love Thine Enemies, etc." and the Ten Commandments were drilled into me. In school and at home our Bill of Rights were paramount in one's education. Freedom of Speech, Freedom and Rights for a fair trial were what our country was all about. Clouds of war descended upon us in 1939 and, with great pride I joined the United State Marine Corps to defend these rights. In one minute after arriving at Parris Island, South Carolina, all those freedoms went right down the tube. You will learn to kill, you will learn to hate the enemy, a superior busts you from Corporal to Private because he decided that you did something wrong and you get penalized many times even though you did absolutely nothing wrong. Ask anyone who went to Boot Camp if they had Freedom of Speech-telling a superior that you did not agree with them-no chance!

By the same token, because of severe discipline, everyone dislikes their drill instructor and yet, when they survive the course, they all admire respect and are appreciative of what the DI didto make them what they are! Think about it! Recruit training had little to do with making you a qualified fighter, an expert rifleman or ready to run the motor pool. Their sole purpose was to make you a Marine, to change you from a Me to a We-to be totally sure that you understood what discipline was all about.

How many times after you left boot camp did you do "left flank march" or got in so many different positions to fire your rifle or had your bed made up to totsl perfection? Playing football, working for a company, going to school- your main consideration is You-Me. Where I stand with the coach, my grades, how I (Me) rank etc. Discipline in the service and particularly in combat, how disciplined the other guys are dictates whether you win or lose and maybe whether you live or die. As a pilot, an infantry person, a sailor on ship, supply or what-have-you, it's a unit or team effort that makes it work.

Your're in a store with your family and one of your kids touches a shelf and knocks over some merchandise-you discipline them but not if some other person does it. You repremand them because you love them and want them to learn what is right. The majority of people on drugs, those who steal, those who cause harm to others, probably were not subjected to the right kind of discipline in their formative years. Love is one of the greatest gifts one can have. But you can not hold it in your hand, buy it at a store or receive it in any way except by giving it to someone else.

#3.

And discipline, and in particular self-discipline is love. You'll enjoy having it!

Addendum D

Quiz.

- You chase what you _____ and run from what you _____.

- If you roughly want to know why you do the things you do, ask yourself what you _____.

- A _____ can make you happy, or unhappy.

- You build the prison, so you have the _____ to it.

- Work hard, work _____.

- Work hard now, or work _____ later.

- Work hard, play _____.

- If it's not _____ you can't distinguish yourself.

- If you have a choice between doing something the hard way or the easy way, the _____ way is usually better, but _____.

- 90 percent of doing something is done in your _____.

- Instead of getting things, one of the quickest ways to increase happiness is to _____ things.

- You already have almost everything you need for everything you _____.

- Life is what you _____ at.

Notes

[1] Reilly, Rick. Twas the Fight Before Christmas. *Sports Illustrated*. December, 1999.

[2] Wachowski, Andy. Wachowski, Lana. *The Matrix*. 1999.

[3] Singer, M.A. (2007). *The untethered soul: The journey beyond yourself*. Oakland, CA: New Harbinger Publications.

[4] The Buddha. An interpretation of *Dhammapada*, verses 153-154.

[5] Cialdini, Robert. (2001). Influence: Science and practice. Boston, MA: Allyn and Bacon.

[6] Nolan, Christopher. (2011). *Inception*.

[7] McCarthy, C. (2006). *The road*. New York: Alfred A. Knopf.

[8] Dawkins, R. The Selfish Gene (New York, New York: Oxford University Press, 1976).

[9] In one experiment, for example, researchers gave subjects $20. For twenty rounds, they asked if subjects wanted to invest $1 on a coin toss. If they lost the coin toss, they lost $1. If they won the coin toss, they won $2.50. The subjects included 15 people with damage to brain parts that control emotions (less emotional subjects), and 19 people without brain damage to brain parts that control emotions (normal subjects).

If you invested every time, you had an 87% chance of making more than $20. Normal subjects invested 58% of the time and earned $22.80 on average. Less emotional subjects with brain damage invested 84% of the time and earned $25.70 on average. Normal subjects also invested significantly less after losing a round than less emotional subjects.

[10] Kahneman, D., Knetsch, J., & Thaler, R. Experimental Test of the endowment effect and the Coase Theorem. *Journal of Political Economy*. 1325-1348 (1990).

[11] Scott, D., Heitzeg, M., Koeppe, R., Stohler, C., & Zubieta, J. Variations in the Human Pain Stress Experience Mediated by Ventral and Dorsal Basal Ganglia Dopamine Activity. *The Journal of Neuroscience*. 10789-10795 (2006).

[12] Berridge, K. C. Pleasures of the brain. *Brain Cogn*. 52, 106-128 (2003).

[13] Leknes, S. & Tracey, I. A Common Neurobiology for Pain and Pleasure. *Nature*. 9, 314-318 (2008).

[14] Barbano, M. & Cador, M. Opioids for hedonic experience and dopamine to get ready for it. *Psychopharmacology*. 191, 497-506 (2007).

[15] Kringelbach, M.L. & Berridge, K.C. The functional neuroanatomy of pleasure and happiness. *Discov Med*. 9, 579-587(2010).

[16] This may not be scientifically correct enough for science, but it's conceptually useful enough for Dad-ence.

[17] Gard, D., Gard, M., Kring, A., & John, O. Anticipatory and consummatory components of the experience of pleasure: a scale development study. *Journal of Research in Personality*. 40, 1086-1102 (2006).

[18] Blake, William. *The Poetical Works of William Blake,* ed. by John Sampson. London, New York: Oxford University Press, 1908.

[19] The band *The Doors* took their name from this 1908 William Blake poem.

[20] Your body produces chemicals that produce pleasure, like adrenaline, dopamine and opioids. You have these chemicals in your body now. If a hyena bursts through your front window your adrenaline

will release and spike.

If we make these pleasure chemicals and have them, why can't we just access and enjoy them? Why can't we simply feel good, without one part of our body having to run off, work hard and bring back bacos to get another part of our body to release opioids?

Imagine if this was possible. Imagine if there was a jellyfish-like creature that could produce and use opioids without having to get anything. It constantly made opioids without input, used them, felt good, and did it again. It never had to do anything other than this.

This creature would be a self-sufficient closed system that wouldn't need a mind or consciousness. What would it need a mind or consciousness for? A mind would not split from the body.

Our bodies need outside input, like food and water, to survive and experience pleasure. We're open systems. The fact that we're required to get these things in hostile landscapes with limited resources favors consciousness.

There may be no point to evolution. Maybe we're not advancing or going anywhere. Why do we have to? For what? For who? We assume that because everything we do has a point, evolution has a point. But does it have to? Maybe life wanders aimlessly. Maybe being just bes. But, in the physical parameters of our system, nature selects for consciousness. Going further, the initial design produced consciousness.

This open system makes us schizophrenic. Our bodies battle our minds. Our bodies want fat, our minds resist. Our minds want youth, our bodies refuse. It's hard to be constrained by the physical needs of entropic bodies. But would we be aware that we had bodies if we weren't?

[21] Greene, R. (2003). *The art of seduction*. New York, N.Y: Penguin.

[22] Whitta, Gary & Shyamalan, M. Night. (2013). *After Earth.*

[23] Shenk, J. (2009). *What Makes Us Happy.* The Atlantic. June 2009.

[24] Schopenhauer, A. (1859). *Die welt als wille und vorstellung.* Leipzig: F.A. Brockhaus.

[25] Thomas, Eric.
https://www.youtube.com/watch?v=WTFnmsCnr6g

[26] Emmerich, Roland. Kloser, Harald. *10,000 B.C.* 2008.

[27] Ness, P. (2008). *The knife of never letting go.* Cambridge, Mass: Candlewick Press.

[28] O'Connor, F. (1962). *Wise blood.* New York: Farrar, Straus and Giroux.

[29] Berridge, K. Wanting and Liking: Observations from the neuroscience and psychology laboratory. *Inquiry.* 378-398 (2009).

[30] Hedonic treadmill. (2015, January 6).
In *Wikipedia, The Free Encyclopedia.* Retrieved 18:50, January 6, 2015,
from http://en.wikipedia.org/w/index.php?title=Hedonic_treadmill&oldid=641208470

[31] O'Doherty, J. et al. Sensory-specific satiety-related olfactory activation of the human orbitofrontal cortex. *Neuroreport* 11, 893–897 (2000).

[32] Everything from this point on I know but frequently can't do. As you know, I get mad, sad and worried. I overthink, yell and lose patience. These tactics, however, help, and may make you "ten percent happier", as Dan Harris smartly said about meditation in his book, Ten Percent Happier; Harris, D. (2014). *10% happier: How I tamed the voice in my head, reduced stress without losing my edge, and found self-help that actually works : a true story.*

---

[33] Nolan, C. (2011). *Inception*.

[34] Palahniuk, C. (1999). *Invisible monsters*. New York: W.W. Norton.

[35] Think of history as if it happened yesterday. Think of today as it will look ten years from now. Think of the future as if it will happen this afternoon, especially when committing to something.

[36] Gautama Buddha. (2015, January 4). In *Wikipedia, The Free Encyclopedia*. Retrieved 15:37, January 4, 2015, from http://en.wikipedia.org/w/index.php?title=Gautama_Buddha&oldid=640928251

[37] Ruiz, M. (1997). *The four agreements: A practical guide to personal freedom*. San Rafael, Calif: Amber-Allen Pub.

[38] Fox, E. (1938). *The Sermon on the Mount: A general introduction to scientific Christianity in the form of a spiritual key to Matthew V, VI and VII*. New York: Harper & Row. Frequently attributed to the Buddha, as detailed by Bodhipaksa: http://www.fakebuddhaquotes.com/holding-onto-anger-is-like-drinking-poison/

[39] Cain, David. (2014). *How to Stop Your Mind from Talking all the Time*. Raptitude.com. http://www.raptitude.com/2014/03/how-to-stop-your-mind-from-talking-so-much/.

[40] Palahniuk, Chuck. (1996). *Fight Club*. New York: W. W. Norton & Company.

[41] Lama, Dalai. *A Human Approach to World Peace*. http://www.dalailama.com/messages/world-peace/a-human-approach-to-peace.

[42] Nolan, Christopher. (2011). *Inception*.

[43] Paraphrased from William James, ""The greatest weapon against stress is our ability to choose one thought over the other."

[44] *Aesop's Fables*. A new translation by Laura Gibbs. Oxford University Press (World's Classics): Oxford, 2002.

[45] Geert van Dijk, *Ainoi, logoi, mythoi: fables in archaic, classical, and Hellenistic Greek*, Brill NL 1997, p.320.

[46] McGovern, M.K. 2002. 2005. *The Effects of Exercise on the Brain.*
http://serendip.brynmawr.edu/bb/neuro/neuro05/web2/m mcgovern.html

[47] Merryman, A., & Bronson, P. (2009). *NutureShock: NEW THINKING ABOUT CHILDREN.*

[48] Miyamoto, Musashi (1974). *A Book of Five Rings*, translated by Victor Harris. London: Allison & Busby; Woodstock, New York: The Overlook Press.

[49] Santideva, Wallace, & Wallace, 1997. http://h-net.msu.edu/cgi-bin/logbrowse.pl?trx=vx&list=h-buddhism&month=0603&week=a&msg=VSX4o5fG5g2wzOArVhua8 A&user=&pw=

[50] Benazir, Ali. What are the Chances of Your Coming Into Being? The Blog of Ali Benazir. 15 June 2011. http://awakenyourgenius.com/

[51]
http://www.newton.dep.anl.gov/askasci/mats05/mats050 57.htm

[52] Lucus, George. Stars Wars. 1974.

[53] NASA, ESA, S. Beckwth (STScl) and the HUDF Team. Http://hubblesite.org/newscenter/archive/releases/20 04/07/image/a/

[54]
http://hubblesite.org/newscenter/archive/releases/20 14/27/image/a/

[55] http://www.nasa.gov/mission_pages/hubble/science/xdf.html

[56] http://hubblesite.org/newscenter/archive/releases/2004/07/image/c/

[57] Along these lines, it takes light from the sun (traveling at 186,000 miles a second) eight minutes to reach your eyeballs. This is how far the sun is from earth. Thus, if the sun exploded, we technically wouldn't see it for eight minutes.

[58] Creighton, Jolene. *Why you should be excited about the James Webb space telescope*. From Quarks to Quasars. 29 June 2014. http://www.fromquarkstoquasars.com/why-you-should-be-excited-about-the-james-webb-space-telescope/

[59] Howell, Elizabeth. *How Many Galaxies are There*. Space.com. 1 April 2014. http://www.space.com/25303-how-many-galaxies-are-in-the-universe.html

[60] "NASA – Galaxy". *NASA and World Book*. Nasa.gov. November 29, 2007. Archived from the original on 2009-04-12. Retrieved 2012-12-06.

[61] Khan, Amina (4 November 2013). "Milky Way may host billions of Earth-size planets". *Los Angeles Times*.

[62] Kaku, Michio (March 2011). *Physics of the Future: How Science Will Shape Human Destiny And Our Daily Lives by the Year 2100*. Doubleday. ISBN 978-0-385-53080-4.

[63] http://en.wikipedia.org/wiki/Wheel

[64] http://www.grc.nasa.gov/WWW/k-12/airplane/atmosphere.html

[65] Federal Aviation Administration (FAA). *Oxygen Equipment; Use in General Aviation Operations*. Section 135.89.

---

http://www.faa.gov/pilots/safety/pilotsafetybrochure
s/media/Oxygen_Equipment.pdf

[66] al-Sharīf, -R. M.-H., 'Alī, . A. T., & In Salmin,
M. A. (1971). *English translation of Nahj-ul-
balagha*. Lahore: Accurate Printers.

[67] NASA, ESA and the Hubble Heritage Team
(STScl/AURA). *A Rose Made of Galaxies Highlights
Hubble's 21st Anniversary.* 20 April 2011.
http://hubblesite.org/newscenter/archive/releases/20
11/11/image/a/

[68] Morley Safer (28 January 2007). "Brain Man". *CBS
News*. Retrieved 2 February 2007

[69] Tammet, Daniel (2006). *Born on a Blue Day*. London:
Hodder & Stoughton.ISBN 978-0-340-89974-8

[70] Gooder, Steve. Channel 4 Documentary. *The Boy
with the Incredible Brain.* 23 May 2005.
https://www.youtube.com/watch?v=z22H89rIMHk

[71] https://www.youtube.com/watch?v=xklinT2g6wU

[72] https://www.youtube.com/watch?v=OWqNoGKJWBI

73 Snyder A., Bahramali H., Hawker T., Mitchell D.J.
2006 Savant-like numerosity skills revealed in
normal people by magnetic
pulses. Perception.35, 837-845. doi:10.1068/p5539.

74

Snyder A.W., Mulcahy E., Taylor J.L., Mitchell D.J., S

achdev P.,Gandevia S.C. 2003 Savant-like skills
exposed in normal people by suppressing the left
fronto-temporal lobe. J. Integr. Neurosci. 2, 149-
158.doi:10.1142/S0219635203000287

75 Gallate J., Chi R., Ellwood S., Snyder A.
2009 Reducing false memories by magnetic pulse
stimulation. Neurosci. Lett. 449, 151-

154.doi:10.1016/j.neulet.2008.11.021.

[76] Snyder A. Explaining and inducing savant skills: privileged access to lower level, less-processed information. Philos Trans R Soc Lond B Biol Sci 2009; 364: 1399-405.

[77] Chi, Richard & Snyder, Allan. Brain stimulation enables the solution of an inherently difficult problem. *Nueroscience Letters*. 121-124 (2012)

[78] Freud, Sigmund. *The Interpretation of Dreams,* Third Edition. Trans. by A. A. Brill. New York: The Macmillan Company, 1913; Bartleby.com, 2010.www.bartleby.com/285/.

[79] Watts, Alan. *Life* magazine (21 April 1961)

[80] Jung, C. Christ, a Symbol of the Self. *Collected Works*. Vol. 9ii. Paragraph 126.

[81] Hampton, C. *A Dangerous Method.* Movie script. Sony Pictures. 2011.

[82] Leung, Rebecca. *Prodigy, 12, Compared to Mozart*. CBS News. 24 November 2004. http://www.cbsnews.com/news/prodigy-12-compared-to-mozart/

[83] Miller, Arthur I. *A Genius Finds Inspiration in the Music of Another.* The New York Times. 31 January 2006.

[84] Einstein, A. (1931). *Cosmic religion: With other opinions and aphorisms*. New York: Covici-Friede.

[85] Tammet, Daniel (2006). *Born on a Blue Day*. London: Hodder & Stoughton.ISBN 978-0-340-89974-8

[86] Kim Peek: savant who was the inspiration for the film Rain Man". *The Times*. 2009-12-23. Retrieved 2009-12-23.

[87]

http://www.lzcenter.com/Myths%20and%20Facts.html

[88] http://www.pbs.org/wgbh/nova/einstein/tiny-answers.html

[89] Wachowski, Andy. Wachowski, Lana. *The Matrix*. 1999.

[90] Pirsig, Robert M. As quoted in *The Book of Bob : Choice Words, Memorable Men* (2007) by Tom Crisp, p. 107.

[91] Hicks, Bill. *Sane Mane*. 1989.

[92] *Bruce Lee: A Warrior's Journey* (2000); here, Lee was reciting lines he wrote for his short lived role on the TV series *Longstreet*

[93] Bhikkhu, Thanissaro. Dvedhavitakka Sutta: Two Sorts of Thinking. 1997.

[94] Einstein, Albert. *How I Constructed the Theory of Relativity*. Kyoto address, 1922. Translated by Masahiro Morikawa from the text recorded in Japanese by Jun Ishiwara, Association of Asia Pacific Physical Societies (AAPPS) Bulletin, Vol. 15, No. 2, pp. 17-19 (April 2005).

[95] Toothman, Jessika. "How Do Humans age in space?". *HowStuffWorks*. Retrieved2012-04-24.

[96] Tolle, Eckhart. *The Power of Now: A Guide to Spiritual Enlightenment*. Novato, CA: New World Library, 1999. Print.

[97] Laozi, ., & Mitchell, S. (1988). *Tao te ching: A new English version.* New York: Harper & Row.

[98] Tolle, E. (1999). *The power of now: A guide to spiritual enlightenment.* Novato, Calif: New World Library.

[99] Tolle, E. (1999). *The power of now: A guide to spiritual enlightenment.* Novato, Calif: New World Library.

[100] Laurant, G., Jeunet, J. *Amelie.* 2001.

[101] Dreyfus, I., & Smith, J. (1896). *Lectures on French literature delivered in Melbourne.* London: Longmans, Green, and Co.

[102] Achor, S. (2010). *The happiness advantage: The seven principles of positive psychology that fuel success and performance at work.* New York: Broadway Books.

[103] Garland E., Froeliger B., Howard M. Neurophysiolocal evidence for remediation of reward processing chronic pain and opioid misuse following treatment with Mindfulness-Orientated Recovery Enhancement: exploratory ERP findings from a pilot RCT. Journal of Behavioral Medicine. 2014.

[104] Scientific American Mind, October/November 2006

[105] Stickgold, Robert, Malia, April; Maguire, Denise; Roddenberry, David; O'Conner, Margaret. *Replaying the Game: Hypnagogic Images in Normals and Amnesics.* Science, October 2000.

[106] R.J. Haier, B.V. Siegel, C. Tang, L. Abel, and M.S. Buchsbaum (1992). *Intelligence*, 16, 415-426.

[107] Ichien, Muju. *Shaseki shu*. 101 Koans compiled in 1283. Translated by Senzaki, Nyogen & Reps, Paul in *101 Zen Stories; Collection of Stone and Sand*. 1940.

Copyright

FIRST EDITION

Kendell E-Pub Edition:
ISBN: **978-0-9961147-0-7**

CreateSpace Paperback Edition:
ISBN: **978-0-9961147-1-4**

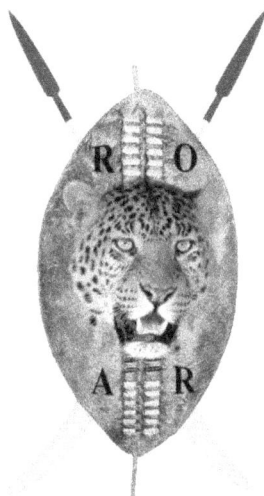

DAD SCHOOL

by: Pop

pop@firebasez.com

Firebase Z
www.firebasez.com